6612

Black
and British
David Bygott

Oxford University Press
1992

Oxford University Press, Walton Street, Oxford OX2 6DP

Oxford New York Toronto
Delhi Bombay Calcutta Madras Karachi
Petaling Jaya Singapore Hong Kong Tokyo
Nairobi Dar es Salaam Cape Town
Melbourne Auckland

and associated companies in

Berlin Ibadan

Oxford is a trade mark of Oxford University Press

© David W. Bygott 1992

ISBN 019 913314 X

A CIP catalogue record for this book is available from the British
Library

Typeset by MS Filmsetting Limited, Frome, Somerset

Printed in Hong Kong

Acknowledgements

The publishers would like to thank the following for
permission to reproduce photographs:

p3 *top left* ITN, *top right* BBC, *bottom* News of the World; p4 *top
centre* Sporting Pictures, *top right* Rod Leon, *bottom right* Laurie
Sparham/Network; p5 *top left* The Guardian/John Chapman;
p5 *middle left* Redferns, *middle right* Ramesh Sharma, *bottom left*
Nottingham Playhouse/Nottingham Evening Post, *bottom right*
Oxford & County Newspapers; p8 *top* Guardian/Martin Argles;
p9 Museum of Antiquities of the University and Society of
Antiquaries of Newcastle-upon-Tyne; p10 Hull City Council
Museums & Art Galleries; p11 National Portrait Gallery, London;
p12 Hull City Council Museums & Art Galleries; p13 Imperial
Tobacco; p14 Hull City Council Museums & Art Galleries; p15
Hulton-Deutsch Collection/The Bettman Archive; p17 Hull City
Council Museums & Art Galleries; p18 The Fotomas Index; p20 *top*
Temple Newsam House, Leeds City Art Galleries, *bottom* Andy
Williams Photo Library; p21 *top* National Portrait Gallery; p21
bottom Bridgeman Art Library/City of Bristol Museum & Art Gallery;
p23 The Board of Trustees of the National Museums and Galleries
on Merseyside (Walker Art Gallery); p24 Mary Evans Picture Library;
p26 *top* The Rt. Hon. The Earl of Mansfield, Scone Palace, Perth,
bottom Mary Evans Picture Library; p27 Bridgeman Art Library/
Royal Albert Memorial Museum, Exeter; p28 *top* Mansell Collection,
bottom Hull City Council Museums & Art Galleries; p29 *top* Hull City
Council Museums & Art Galleries, *bottom* Photostage; p31 Mary
Evans Picture Library; p32 The Board of Trustees of the National
Musems and Galleries on Merseyside (Walker Art Gallery); p33 Mary
Evans Picture Library; p35 Hulton-Deutsch Collection; p36 Photo
R.M.N./Versailles; p39 National Portrait Gallery, London; p41
Camera Press; p42 *left* Sefton Photo Library; p43 *top* Andrew Wiard
(Report/IFL Archive), *bottom* National Portrait Gallery Library/The
Conway Library, Courtauld Institute of Art; p44 National Portrait
Gallery, London; p45 The Board of Trustees of the National
Museums and Galleries on Merseyside (Liverpool Museum); p47
Sidney Harris; p48 Imperial War Museum, London; p50 *top*
Universal Pictorial Press, *bottom* Allsport/Adrian Murrell; p52
Hulton-Deutsch; p53 *top* Val Wilmer/Format, *bottom* Val Wilmer/
Format; p54 *top* Hulton-Deutsch; p55 Press Association; p56 Kobal
Collection/Korda; p57 *top* Kobal Colection/Columbia, *bottom left*
The Guardian/Frank Martin, *bottom right* Ramesh Sharma; p58 *left*
Gowan/Network, *right* Hansib Publishing Ltd; p60 *top* Christine
Osborne Pictures; p61 Caroline Rees; p62 The Guardian/Frank
Martin; p63 Hulton-Deutsch Collection; p64 *top* The Guardian/
Graham Turner, *left* The Guardian/Don Mcphee; p66 Laurie
Sparham/Network; p68 David Hoffman; p69 Ramesh Sharma; p70
top Ramesh Sharma, *bottom* Network; p71 *top* The Guardian,
bottom John Sturrock/Network; p72 The Guardian/Don McPhee;
p74 *top* Redferns, *bottom* BBC; p75 *top* Bob Thomas Sports
Photography, *bottom* AP/Stephen Holland; p76 *top* Universal
Pictorial Press, *bottom* Press Association; p79 Press Association.

Although every effort has been made to trace and contact copyright
holders before publication, we have not been successful in a few
cases. If notified, the publishers will be pleased to rectify any
omissions at the earliest opportunity.

Introduction

The history of the people who live in Britain is a patchwork of stories of countless newcomers, some of them brutal invaders, some of them peaceful immigrants, who came to these shores at different times and stayed. Most were white, some were black. In this book, we focus on the history of just one grouping within Britain's black community, namely those whose family roots may be traced back to Africa via the Caribbean: the Afro-Caribbeans.

At the beginning of the 1990s they made up just under one per cent of the British population. The majority of them were born in Britain. Most were English or Welsh, some were Scots. Because of their ancestry they might also find themselves referred to as 'West Indians'.

The 1979 Conservative Party manifesto noted:

> 66 The ethnic minorities have already made a valuable contribution to the life of our nation. 99

In the 1980s, an increasing number of Britain's black citizens achieved success in areas where once only whites were to be seen. In 1981 Roland Butcher (born in Barbados) became the first Afro-Caribbean to play cricket for England; Wilfred Wood, from Barbados, became Britain's first black Church of England bishop in 1985; in 1987 London-born Diane Abbott was the first black woman to become a Member of Parliament; in 1988 Richard Stokes joined the previously all-white Grenadier Guards; in 1989 Jamaican-born Tony Robinson, a retired bus-driver, became the first black Sheriff of Nottingham; and so on. In this book, we explore the background to these 'firsts', we look at some of the achievements that came long before them, and we see how even in the 1990s, after black people have lived in this country for centuries, few have reached positions of any great power in society, and racism remains an everyday danger.

Official estimates for the late 1980s put Britain's 'West Indian or Guyanese' population at 494,600 (out of a total UK population of 54,519,000) and put its 'African' population at 112,000. Most were of working age and in work or seeking work. About 25 per cent were aged under 16. Only 7 per cent were 60 or over.

Two of the most familiar faces on British TV: top newsreaders Trevor McDonald and Moira Stuart. McDonald, who was born in Trinidad, became Britain's first black TV newsreader; and Stuart soon followed in 1981.

WINNER John Barnes, a hero for England

John Barnes (b. Jamaica, 1963), a Liverpool and England football star. He was the first black footballer to be chosen as Britain's Footballer of the Year – in 1987/88 and again in 1989/90. In *Out of his skin: the John Barnes Phenomenon* (1989) D. Hill wrote: 'When Barnes gets the ball at his feet ... he does more than merely threaten to score – he carries with him the hope of not just a better game, but a better nation too'. On 11 June 1984 the *Sun* newspaper called John Barnes 'a hero for England'.

1 Defining terms

Black people ...

❝... are really just like everybody else. Some of them are exceptional and most of them are not.❞

James Baldwin (1924–87)

In 1989 Stephen Wiltshire published *Cities*, his second book of drawings; and the second exhibition of his work opened in London. 15 years old and autistic, Stephen was judged by Sir Hugh Casson to be 'possibly the best child artist in Britain'.

Right: Jennifer Stoute, running for Great Britain.

Below: Jamaican-born Valerie Ricketts was not only elected to Oxford City Council but opened Oxford's premier Caribbean restaurant in 1988.

Of the 650 Members of Parliament elected in 1987, four were black. Two of these were this country's first MPs of Afro-Caribbean descent: Londoner Diane Abbott (see page 43) and Guyanese-born Bernie Grant.

Right: At the Notting Hill carnival in 1980.

This street in Brixton is named after Marcus Garvey. He was born in Jamaica in 1887 and died in Britain in 1940. He did not fulfil his grandest dreams – but his campaigning, particularly in the USA, lifted the hearts of millions of blacks and strengthened them in their struggle for justice and equality.

In 1989 Claire Holder, a barrister who went to school in Trinidad and once played in a steel band, took over as chief organiser of the Notting Hill Carnival.

Trinidadian-born Billy Ocean's song 'Caribbean Queen' (1984) was the first hit by a black British performer to top the US black singles chart.

Right: A conversation during a demonstration in London, May 1983.

Left: At Christmas 1989 Clive Rowe from Lancashire was playing Widow Twankey in the pantomime *Aladdin*. 'It's going to take time for black actors to be fully accepted, but it's happening', he said.

In 1990 Dr Maureen Davis, a chemical engineer with British Gas, was a finalist in the Women of Tomorrow competition.

I'M REALLY PUZZLED, BEV. I DON'T KNOW WHAT TO CALL YOU. WEST INDIAN? BLACK? AFRO? AFRO-CARIBBEAN?

JUST CALL ME BEV. O.K?

What is 'black'?

The word 'black' is often used today, and with pride, to refer to anyone in Britain who is not 'white'. 'Black' may mean people who are descended from Africans, Maoris, Indians, Pakistanis or Chinese, for example. The term is used most widely, however, to refer to people of African or part-African descent, including Afro-Caribbeans.

Over the centuries, whites in Europe have used lots of different labels to describe those with darker skins. In ancient Greece and Rome, blacks from any part of Africa were referred to as 'Ethiopians' or 'Moors'. Similarly, in an account of a long voyage, published in 1578, an English sea-captain, George Best, wrote:

66 (A Biblical curse affected) these blacke
Moores which are in Africa (and was)
the cause of ye Ethiopians blacknesse. 99

In fact, as we now know, people with dark skins simply have more of a pigment called melanin in their skins than others. This substance gives some protection against dangerous ultra-violet rays of the sun.

Once, the word 'Negro' was in fashion. In 1596 Elizabeth I wrote of the 'great number of negars and Blackamoors' living in her kingdom. Both 'Negro' and 'negar' come from the Latin word for black, 'niger', after which the River Niger and Nigeria are named. In its form 'nigger' it is used as an insult, so this was banned by the BBC before World War II.

'Coloured', once a common term, was always an odd choice, for everybody is coloured. A quick comparison with a sheet of white paper shows that even so-called 'whites' have skin that contains colour. Some are very pale, of course, but most are somewhat pink!

In the 1960s, during a huge drive for equal rights in the USA – in which some blacks of West Indian ancestry were prominent, including Stokely Carmichael and Malcolm X – the word 'black' became popular. It had been used in Tudor times, too (and in seventeenth century Britain it had included servants from India). But now it was used by many blacks with pride, as in the phrase: 'black is beautiful'.

The term 'immigrant' is often used nowadays. But it does not apply to most Afro-Caribbeans in Britain. At a meeting of trade unionists in Cardiff in 1991, the General Secretary of the Transport and General Workers Union, Ron Todd, looked forward to society 'in which racism and its myths are dead forever' and said:

66 Our black and ethnic minority
communities have deep roots in this
society. As you all know, black people
have lived in Tiger Bay, for example, for
200 years or more. They are not
immigrants – not in any sense that I
understand. We have to be quite clear
in the words we use. Such language
was out of place even 20 years ago, let
alone today. They are British; they are
here to stay; they are a vital part of
society. 99

Similarly, in September 1991 John Major, the British Prime Minister said to a group of black students at a meeting of the Windsor Fellowship;

66 I regard any barrier built upon race as
pernicious – all the more so as black
and Asian people have lived in this
country for a long time. I hope you can
say you are black, British and Windsor
Fellows, and are proud of all three. 99

Not Biblical, after all

In 1988 Pope John Paul II issued a document called *The Church and Racism*. In it he spoke of 'the unity of humankind'. He described 'every form of discrimination based on race' as unacceptable. He declared the idea that the Bible sees Africans as inferior to be 'false interpretation'.

Why 'West Indies?'

Anyone new to the history of Britain's Afro-Caribbeans would do well to know where the Caribbean is and consider what the term 'West Indian' means.

The West Indies is the name of a 4,000 km long archipelago (a chain of islands) in the Caribbean Sea (see map). The islands are mostly of volcanic origin and tropical in climate, with a wide variety of plant life. There are three main groups of islands: the Bahamas, the Lesser Antilles and the Greater Antilles (which include Cuba, Hispaniola, Puerto Rico and Jamaica). The 'West Indies' is not just one single country. Some areas are still colonies, such as the Caymans, which are British. Some islands were once Spanish, French or Dutch and the US Virgin Isles once belonged to the Danes.

The name 'West Indies' came about some 500 years ago, when the explorer Christopher Columbus mistakenly thought he had reached part of Asia. It is a term that continues to cause confusion today. In Britain, some 8,000 km away, people often think that is refers only to places that have been British colonies. As you can see from the map, this ignores the two biggest islands, Cuba and Hispaniola. The 'West Indies' may include Guyana or Belize (formerly British Honduras) which are on the mainland of South and Central America, and Bermuda, which is not in the Caribbean at all.

The population of the West Indies is richly varied. There are black people descended from Africans (who make up the majority in Jamaica, for example, though its name 'Xaymaca' came from the Arawak natives who once lived here). Many people are of nineteenth century Asian origin; 'East Indians' were brought from India to work in the Caribbean. There are whites with origins in Europe (who form the majority in Cuba). Many others come from marriages between groups and, for example, in Dominica or Aruba, there are a few descendants of the Carib natives whose name gave rise to the word Caribbean. Clearly, not all West Indians are Afro-Caribbean – the two terms do not mean the same.

Some surveys of Britain's population include as West Indian both (a) people who moved here from the West Indies and (b) their children – even if the children were born in Britain. But today's British-born black youth, while respecting their ancestry, rarely call themselves West Indian. If a label has to be used, they prefer Afro-Caribbean, African, African-Caribbean black or Black British. Or simply 'British'!

> **Still true today?**
> In a novel called *The Lonely Londoners*, published in 1956, Trinidadian-born Samuel Selvon wrote about a character called Moses:
> 'Now Moses don't know a damn thing about Jamaica – Moses come from Trinidad, which is a thousand miles from Jamaica, but the English people believe that everybody who come from the West Indies come from Jamaica'.

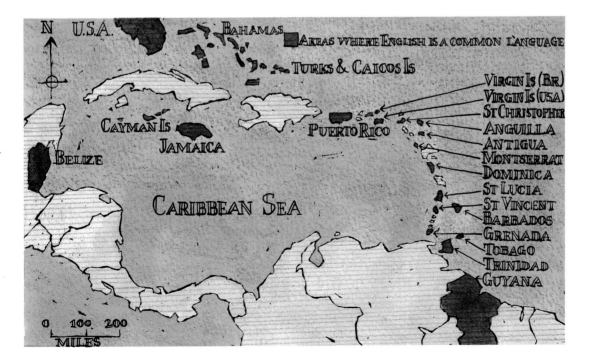

African roots

In this book we focus mainly on the past five centuries. Yet the roots of Afro-Caribbeans stretch back in time, beyond the mighty kingdoms of Mali, Songhay or Benin, to the ancient civilisations of Nubia or Cush that built pyramids and cities many centuries before the Romans set out to civilise Britain. Egypt is in Africa and it had pharaohs who were black. Aristotle viewed Egypt's priests as the inventors of geometry, arithmetic and astronomy; and Greek scholars such as Eudoxos travelled to Egypt to study.

If this is not common knowledge, it is because more recently the achievements of others have been centre stage. Since 1589 it has been possible to read in Hakluyt's *Voyages* how Thomas Wyndham arrived in Benin in 1553 to be offered 80 tons of pepper *on credit* or to read of John Lok's return to London in 1555 with a cargo that included a large quantity of gold. But modern eyes have been on those who colonised Africa, not on pre-colonial history. Frantz Fanon, who was born in the West Indies in 1924, wrote that colonists are not content to rule the present but try to destroy 'the past of the oppressed people', and in the days of Empire many whites did look on Africans as children, with no history of note. At best faint praise was offered, as in this toast from a poem by Rudyard Kipling:

> **❝**So 'ere's to you, Fuzzy-Wuzzy,
> at your 'ome in the Soudan;
> You're a pore benighted 'eathen
> but a first-class fightin' man.**❞**

The claim some people made – that Africans were happier as slaves in the New World than when free in Africa – was dismissed as propaganda by an Afro-Caribbean, C. L. R. James, in *The Black Jacobins* (1938).

> **❝**In the sixteenth century Central Africa was a territory of peace and happy civilisation. Traders travelled thousands of miles from one side of the continent to another without molestation. The tribal wars from which the European pirates claimed to deliver the people were mere sham-fights; it was a great battle when half-a-dozen men were killed.**❞**

However, even today, for some, African history still begins when the continent was discovered by Britain!

The Trinidadian-born historian and cricket writer C. L. R. James (1901–89).

In 1918 John Archer (see page 45) said: 'We have a history to be proud of ... before Romulus founded Rome, before Homer sang, when Greece was in its infancy, Meroe was the chief city of the Negroes along the Nile. Its private and public buildings, its markets and public squares ..., its inventive genius and ripe scholarship, made it the cradle of civilisation and the mother of art. It was the queenly city of Ethiopia. Egypt borrowed her light from the venerable Negroes up the Nile. Greece went to school to the Egyptians, and Rome turned to Greece. Thus the flow of civilisation has been from the East, the place of light, to the West.'

The result of modern research

I am very dubious of the utility of the concept 'race' in general because it is impossible to achieve any anatomical precision on the subject. Nevertheless, I am convinced that, at least for the last 7,000 years, the population of Egypt has contained African, South-West Asian and Mediterranean types. I believe that Egyptian civilization was fundamentally African and that the African element was stronger in the Old and Middle Kingdoms. Furthermore, I am convinced that many of the most powerful Egyptian dynasties which were based in Upper Egypt – the 1st, 11th, 12th and 18th – were made up of pharaohs whom one can usefully call black.

Professor M. Bernal, Black Athena (1987)

2 In ships to 'Babylon'

Early records

The first blacks in Britain may have been those who came here 2,000 years ago with the Roman Imperial Army, long before the Angles or the Saxons arrived. Most of these blacks were Berbers or Moors from northern Africa. Some of them were personal servants or slaves (along with many whites). Other blacks were soldiers. Roman records refer to a body of 'Moors' defending Hadrian's Wall, for example, in the far north of England.

After the Roman occupation ended, some Romans stayed on, settling permanently. Were any of these people black? Were their children the first blacks born in Britain? Evidence is scarce. Some male skeletons found in a Romano-British cemetery in Yorkshire have proportions which, some think, indicate African descent. The same is thought of the remains of a young girl buried in the ninth century in Norfolk. But it is difficult for archaeologists to identify an ethnic group solely by examining ancient bones.

It is not until the end of the fifteenth century that we can be certain of a continuous black presence in Britain. Certainly, there were blacks in Britain from early Tudor times. Black musicians were playing at the royal courts of both. England and Scotland as the sixteenth century began. We do not know how long they had been there. The Portuguese started to ship African captives to Europe in the fifteenth century, some of whom were given new non-African names and supplied as exotic 'novelties' to entertain rich families. Was this the case in Britain, too?

The name of the black musician drumming in Edinburgh for James IV of Scotland in 1505 is not known. The name of the black trumpeter who played for Henry VII of England and later Henry VIII is given in the wages accounts of 1507 as John Blanke (meaning 'John White'). But nothing is known of either musician's origins.

In Edinburgh with the drummer were his wife, their baby and some other blacks, one of whom was christened on 11 December 1504. The Queen had two black servants, Ellen and Margaret, and court records show that in 1513, on New Year's day, gifts of ten French crowns were made 'to the twa blak ledeis'.

Clothes bills refer to 'blak Margaret' and 'Elen More', and in 1527 a payment was made to 'Helenor, the blak moir'. In some old texts the word 'blak' simply means dark-haired, but here the words 'More' and 'moir' clearly point to Africa.

This tombstone, from South Shields, records how Victor, 'by nation a Moor', had served a cavalryman, Numerianus, become a free man, and died young.

Slaves were branded like cattle with red-hot irons, as in this nineteenth-century painting by A. F. Biard.

New ships, new cargo

The increasing evidence of black people in Tudor Britain comes from an age in which great advances in technology were being made. Better ships that could sail on the open ocean and better navigation allowed 'new' worlds to be explored. The new ships could also transport slaves over long distances.

Pioneering seafarers from Spain and Portugal had set out to explore the coastline of Africa. They were trying to find a sea-route to the spices of the East and to Ethiopia (which had been a source of gold by overland routes for thousands of years. Sailing south beyond the Canaries and Cape Bojadur – which many believed marked the edge of the world, over which any explorer must plunge to death –

was not for the faint-hearted. In 1441 a ship returned with twelve captured West Africans. The tears of the next 235 arrivals, in 1444, were recalled by a courtly eye-witness, Gomes Eannes de Azurara, in his *Chronicle of Guinea*. But to Pope Nicholas V these blacks were heathens; and in 1452 he authorised the Portuguese to conquer and enslave any other heathens in Guinea.

For a long time, England's ships were no match for the caravels of Portugal. However, English merchants took note as they saw the wealth of West Africa brought out in the form of pepper grains, ivory, gold and 'black gold' – slaves. They noted, too, the growing demand for slaves in the new Spanish colonies in Brazil and the Caribbean, where the settlers wanted ever more people to toil in gold mines and plantations. Fortunes could be made by supplying slaves – if you had a good ship and a tough crew.

New merchants

Sending ships into the Mediterranean or to the Canary Isles was risky enough for some English merchants. There were storms, disease, pirates and, in addition, the problem of foreign languages. They hesitated to trade with a

---

Name: blank

Black slaves had to give up their names. It cut them off from their past, and it must have hurt especially if they were given a name that mocked them, such a Caesar, Pompey or Dido. In 1952 an African-American called Malcolm Little (the son of a Baptist preacher and a woman from Grenada whose father was a white man) changed his name to Malcolm X. The X symbolised his unknown African name.

---

region they did not know. It took a man called John Lok to tempt them. In 1555 he returned from West Africa with a cargo of gold, the head of an elephant, and five Africans who could act as 'linguisters' [interpreters]. After that it was not long before the first English sea-captain engaged in the slave trade: a young white man from Plymouth called John Hawkins.

Hawkins set sail for Guinea in 1562. Since Africans had been kidnapped and shipped to the 'New World' for half a century now, he would have heard how the deed was done. Crews with guns went ashore and captured any young blacks they met. Sometimes local African rulers helped by capturing blacks from other areas and selling them to the slavers in return for goods from Europe, rather than risk being captured and sold themselves.

When offered slaves in Africa in 1620, one ship's captain, Richard Jobson said:

66 We are a people who do not deal in such commodities. We do not buy and sell one another, nor any creatures that bear human form. 99

But it was the example set by Hawkins and his cousin Francis Drake that the nation followed. Gradually, Britain developed into the world's major slave-trading nation.

The 'Atlantic triangle'

John Hawkins' voyage of 1562–3 took him thousands of kilometres. The voyage consisted of three stages or 'passages'.

First, with a cargo of goods from England that would be in short supply in Africa, he sailed to Sierra Leone. There, according to Richard Hakluyt, in *The Principall Navigations, Voiages and Discoveries of the English Nation*:

66 (Hawkins) stayed some good time and got into his possession, partly by the sworde, and partly by other meanes, to the number of 300 Negros at the least. 99

Branded with hot irons and chained together, the prisoners were forced on board Hawkins' ship and crammed together below deck. Then Hawkins set off on the 'middle passage' of his voyage, transporting his victims 8,000 kilometres across the Atlantic to the Caribbean island of Hispaniola. Here, Spanish colonists wanted more labourers for their expanding plantations; so Hawkins was able to sell his prisoners for a high price. This allowed him to buy a third cargo – cane sugar, spices, hides and pearls – wanted by people in Europe.

If any Africans had managed to stay on board, by stowing away, hoping to return to

This portrait of John Hawkins (1532–95) hangs in the National Portrait Gallery, London. (Not one portrait of a black is displayed there.)

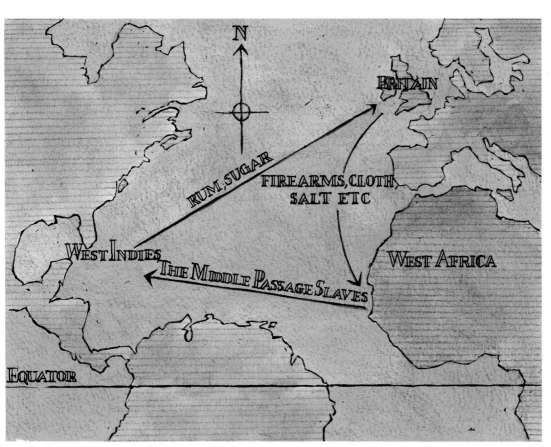

their homeland on the ship that had taken them away, they must have been disappointed. For now Hawkins set sail to sell his final cargo in England.

Ships that sailed the 'Atlantic triangle' never sailed empty. On each leg of his voyage Hawkins made a profit. Everyone he traded with gained, too. Hawkins left home carrying a respectable cargo and came home with another one. Who in England cared if, on the way, some people had lost everything?

The middle passage

As many fit, young Africans as possible were packed into the slave-ships' holds. They were given no bedding but had to sleep on bare wooden boards. In the course of a rough passage that lasted two to three months the skin on their elbows might be chafed to the bone. They had to cope with the dark, cramped conditions, with sickness, grief and fear. They were allowed on deck for fresh air for only a few minutes per day. One in six people died.

One man who did survive the middle passage (see page 27) wrote in *The Interesting Life of Olaudah Equiano or Gustavus Vassa* (1789):

66One day, when we had a smooth sea and moderate wind, two of my wearied countrymen who were chained together, preferring death to such a life of misery, somehow made through the nettings and jumped into the sea. Immediately, another quite dejected fellow, who on account of his illness was suffered (allowed) to be out of irons, also followed their example. I believe many more would soon have done the same if they had not been prevented by the ship's crew, who were instantly alarmed. Those of us that were the most active were in a moment put under the deck, and there was such a noise and confusion amongst the people of the ship to stop her and get the boat out to go after the slaves as I never heard before. However, two of the wretches were drowned, but they got the other, and afterwards flogged him unmercifully for thus attempting to prefer death to slavery.99

Part of the loading-plan of a Liverpool slave-ship, the *Brookes*. Measurements taken in 1788 by a Royal Navy captain showed each slave was allotted a coffin-sized space, about 180 cm by 40 cm by 80 cm high.

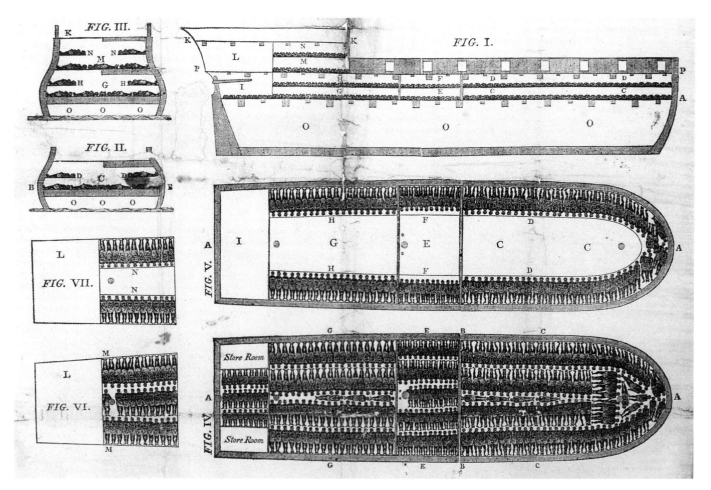

A growing sea power

When John Hawkins returned to England in 1563, he did not conceal what he had done in his search for fortune. On the contrary, he advertised his new trade in a redesigned coat-of-arms showing a shackled black man. Nor was he treated as an outcast by English high society (who soon found it amusing to have a black slave or servant in their homes). And Elizabeth I's reaction? She loaned Hawkins one of her own ships, the *Jesus*. Hawkins was able to set off in 1564 on a second slave-trading trip, returning a year later to share his profits with the Queen.

Hawkins' third voyage to Guinea and the Caribbean was in 1567–69. This time he led six ships, one captained by his younger cousin, Francis Drake (who had made a similar trip in 1566). Again, Hawkins sold slaves to Spanish colonists; but he also raided their settlements and ships and so angered the King of Spain.

Like many who profited from the slave trade, Hawkins became an MP and was later knighted. More significantly, he took over from his father-in-law as Treasurer of the Navy, which he strengthened and modernised. In 1588 Hawkins was third-in-command of the fleet that fought the Spanish Armada (Drake was second-in-command). Without their experience and knowledge of the sea, the English fleet might not have grown to command the world's sea-ways and, through them, its trade.

Both Hawkins and Drake died in the Caribbean during a joint expedition to raid Spanish silver ships in 1595–96.

More colonies, more slaves

In Hawkins' lifetime, tens of thousands of Africans were transported across the Atlantic. Then, in the seventeenth century even more, when new colonies were established in North America and the West Indies (including St Kitts, Barbados, Montserrat, Antigua, Jamaica, the Caymans, the Turks and Caicos Islands, the Bahamas and the Virgins).

In St Kitts, tobacco and indigo were planted. Soon it was Africans who were out in the fields tending the crops. In Barbados, slaves produced 'white gold' (sugar) and the rum that was made from it. Whatever crop was grown in the new colonies – sugar cane, ginger, rice or cotton – the trade in slave workers grew. In Barbados there were 5,680 African slaves in 1645, but by 1667 there were 82,023.

What was the total number of Africans transported? We do not know. Most of Britain's

An early advertisement for tobacco.

slave-ships sailed from Liverpool and Bristol, but many sailed from London too (from 1698 to 1807 on average one every fortnight). Ships kept inventories of their cargoes, but these were not always correct. Smuggling was common especially where taxes were charged on all incoming cargoes. By the mid-nineteenth century, according to the estimate of Leopold Senghor (President of Senegal 1960–80), up to 20 million had been transported, while for each one taken, perhaps ten more died. In *How Europe Underdeveloped Africa*, 1974 the Guyanese historian Walter Rodney wrote:

> 66 No-one knows for certain how many Africans were taken from their homes to be slaves, but it has been estimated that more than 15,000,000 Africans reached the American continent and the Caribbean islands. It is not surprising, therefore, to find that many historians suggest that, altogether, West Africa lost 40–50,000,000 people. 99

In 1663, with the king and queen again financing the slave trade, a new coin was struck. Made from the gold of West Africa, it was to measure Britain's wealth for a century and a half – until Britain stopped trading in slaves. It might have been called the 'West Africa'. In fact it was called the Guinea.

A slave's life

> “Sometimes I feel like a motherless child,
> a long way from home.”

The planters across the Atlantic paid best for fit and strong youths. The old and the sick were left behind to see their villages and crops burn, and their children taken away – again and again. The effect on Africa was crippling. Once in the Caribbean the kidnapped people were

a) forbidden to speak their own languages – they had to learn pidgin (simple) English;
b) made to answer to a non-African name, chosen for them by their new 'owner';
c) forbidden to practise their traditional religions (they were taught that Christian obedience in this world would bring its rewards in the next world);
d) introduced to a slave's work.

Names	Employment and Charracter	Price Appraised
Infants	Amount Brought forward	£ 2900
Catto	Infant	30
Adam	d°	20
Stephen	d°	15
Christianas	d° About A Year Old	10
Women		
Mimba	At Nurse well disposed and may be depended on	110
Molly	Infirm attends the overseer	46
Margaret	Able field well disposed and a Distiller	100
Lyddia	Old Weakley but Constant field Negroe	65
Clarrissa	Able field Negroe and Constant	90
Dolly	Able field Negroe with Child	100
Juba Warner	d° Constant	91
Nanny	Weekly but Constant field Negroe	72
Patience	Elderly field Negroe	50
Ophelia	field Negroe Infirm but with Child	77
Juba	Able field Negroe	110
Penny	Ditto	87
Sylvia	Ditto	110
Sarah	Ditto	91
Susannah	Ditto	110
Betsey	Ditto	105
Margritta	Ditto	110
Coomba	Ditto	112
Lucy	Follows Grass Gang has A Swelled Leg	46
Dianna	Able field Negroe	110
Betty	Ditto	87
Fanny	Ditto	100
Sally	Constant but Weekly Ditto	81
Hannah	Able field apt to Runaway	75
Marcy	Young field Negroe	101
Betty	d° but Apt Runaway	69
Grace	Young field Negroe	76
Penda Creol	Ditto	108
Girls		

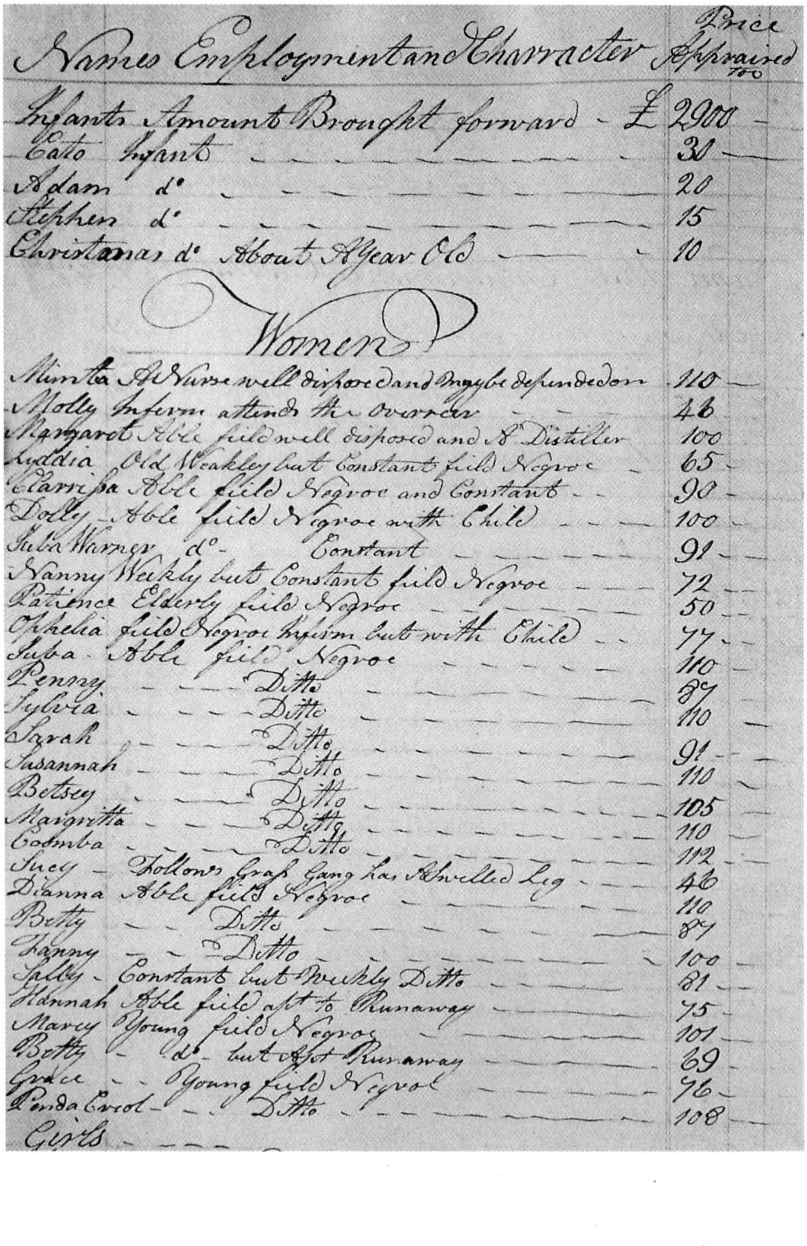

A page from the inventory of Valley Plantation, St John's, Jamaica, 1787.

The cane-fields were hacked from jungle in hot, tropical lowland areas. Here, slaves toiled up to 18 hours a day, then grew their own food in their spare time. To cut cane, they did not need to read or write, so they were not taught. Many who tried to learn were flogged – in Jamaica with a whip three metres long. Why? Because they might read things that would give them ideas or forge documents, setting themselves free!

Jamaica's slave population rose from 45,000 in 1700 to 200,000 by 1784. Yet in that time over 600,000 had arrived. It was no less than murder.

Workers wanted, not families

Slavery did not just mean work. It also destroyed human bonds. Relatives or friends who survived the middle passage together were auctioned off separately. Or planters could use the threat of an auction to make a slave obedient. Any new family formed in captivity could be broken up at once. Husbands were split up from wives and children from parents, with little hope of hearing from each other ever again. The autobiographies of former slaves testify to the heart-break and terror that they faced. Josiah Henson recalled how, when he was only five years old:

> “My brothers and sisters were bid off first, one by one, while my mother, paralyzed by grief held me by the hand. Her turn came, and she was bought. Then I was offered to the assembled purchasers.”

No slave could ever ever go to sleep at night certain of not being sold to a new 'owner' the next morning.

The price of disobedience

Until the mid-eighteenth century 'seasoned slaves', who had survived the harsh, initial breaking-in period in the West Indies, were regularly shipped north to America and re-auctioned at a higher price. Among the slave-holders there were numerous US Presidents, including George Washington, Thomas Jefferson, Andrew Jackson and John Tyler. But one in four slaves did not live long enough for that. Punishment for opposing a planter's will was savage.

A white doctor, Sir Hans Sloane, sailed to the Caribbean in 1686 and visited Barbados, Nevis, St Kitts and Jamaica. In a journal of his voyage, *Natural History of Jamaica*, he observed:

> **66** Burning them by nailing them down on the ground with crooked sticks on every limb and then applying the Fire by degrees from the feet and hands, burning them gradually up to the head. For crimes of lesser nature Gelding, or chopping off half of the foot with an Axe. For negligence, they are usually whipt by the overseer with Lance-wood Switches, till they be bloody. After they are whip'd till they are raw, some put on their skins Pepper and Salt to make them smart. **99**

A source of strength

African slaves in British colonies were not allowed to follow any religion other than Christianity. Eventually, this was to become a source of strength. At first it meant little.

Slaves were often refused baptism, for example; this was because planters thought 'heathens' could be slaves but were not sure of the legal position if their slaves were to be christened. Would that automatically set them free?

Ottobah Cugoano, remembering his days as a slave in Grenada, wrote in 1787:

> **66** I saw a slave receive twenty-four lashes of the whip for being seen in church on a Sunday instead of going to work. **99**

Some planters made no exception even when Christmas Day fell on a Sunday. Others sent their slaves to church, but kept them well away from white worshippers. The pattern varied. Some slaves were able to build their own Christian church and have their own deacons, who might be freed blacks.

Blacks arriving from a different colony sometimes brought new traditions. In 1784 George Liele, a Baptist ex-slave from America, preached to large congregations in the Kingston area of Jamaica. Missionaries came too, often to stress the need for obedience, but not always. One white missionary, John Smith, was convicted of aiding a revolt in Guyana in 1823. He died in prison.

Some aspects of Christianity appealed to slaves at once: the just and loving God who was more powerful than a white planter; universal brotherhood; the prospect of Judgement Day, when whites, too, would face their creator; the Old Testament story of how Moses led the children of Israel out of slavery in Babylon; and the tradition of hymns. This last aspect was very valuable. While slaves were punished savagely if they criticised their 'masters' openly, they could hardly be stopped from singing songs based on Biblical events. So, as formerly in Africa, with a soloist to lead, and a chorus to join in, the slaves sang songs that expressed their feelings and told their history. These songs – known as gospel music, Negro spirituals or Sorrow Songs – said a great deal about their own situation as slaves. Obvious examples include '*Go down, Moses*' and '*Ev'rybody got to die*'. This tradition carries on in black musical styles. The first reggae song to be played on US radio stations was a Desmond Dekker hit. It went to No. 1 in Britain in March 1969 – its title was *The Israelites*.

The power of humour

In their struggle to survive, slaves told folktales, too, about creatures who had secret powers or seemed weak but outsmarted others more powerful. They also told jokes that mocked their troubles and were both funny and sad at the same time. Based on experience and often self-mocking, they showed a spirit able to soar above temporary troubles – a spirit still alive in the twentieth century. J. R. Archer, for example, told the story of a white woman who wanted to marry a black man, but wasn't sure how her clergyman brother would react. So the black man checked. 'I heard you say in the pulpit last Sunday, "God hath made of one blood all nations on the earth to dwell".' 'Yes', the white man said , 'and I'll do so again next Sunday. I don't object to your being my brother in Christ, I just object to your being my brother-in-law'.

In 1873 the Fisk Jubilee Singers toured Britain, singing gospel music. Most members of the choir had been slaves in the USA. Now, they introduced their audiences, including Queen Victoria, to *Steal away to Jesus, Nobody knows the trouble I see* and *Swing low, sweet chariot.*

3 | Why was slavery accepted?

Blacks fought back

Anyone not familiar with black history must wonder why blacks accepted slavery. They did not, of course. No matter what punishments were carried out, or how many harsh laws were passed by whites to control them, blacks still rebelled. Despite the message of humility that was preached to them, Africans were not always eager to smile and obey. Far from it. They fought back in many ways, both directly and indirectly. In the struggle to end slavery, black people were always in the front line.

- Some refused to be slaves and took their own lives. Sometimes pregnant women preferred abortion to bringing a child into slavery.

- Most tried to slow the pace of work by shamming illness or stupidity, causing fires or breaking tools 'accidentally'.

- Whenever possible, slaves ran away. But escaping was easier than staying free. With no papers to prove they had been freed legally, they could not go to a different area, under a new name, and look for paid work. Being black, they were immediately recognised as runaways and were returned to be punished by their 'owners'. Some escaped to South America or, later, to England or parts of North America where there was no slavery. Each such act of courage struck a blow against slavery as a whole: for it made the business less profitable. Planters were faced with the cost of a chase or the expense of buying and training a replacement.

- Slaves in some areas ran, then fought. After England took Jamaica from Spain in 1655, many slaves fled inland to the Cockpit hills and set up free communities in the dense forests. For a century, these 'maroons' (from the Spanish *ci-marron* meaning 'wild') used guerilla tactics to harass the whites. One legendary maroon leader gave her name to Nanny Town in the Blue Mountains.

- Unarmed slaves had to be brave to fight overseers with guns or the trained army that could be called in. Yet on top of countless acts by individuals came hundreds of revolts on a far larger scale. For example, in Barbados in 1675, after which six rebels were burned alive and 11 beheaded; Antigua in 1687, when one rebel was burned to death and another had his tongue torn out as an 'Example to the rest'; Antigua in 1735–36, after which 77 were burned alive and six starved to death on gibbets; Jamaica, 1760; Dominica constantly; Grenada in 1795–96 (under Julien Fédon, who was never captured, although once he only got away by leaping over the edge of a cliff); St Lucia in 1796–97; Barbados again in 1816....

- One revolt, encouraged by the French Revolution, began in 1791 in the French colony of St Domingue. It was led by Toussaint l'Ouverture, the grandson of an African chief, and kept going until the blacks were free and in charge. In his vivid account of the revolt, *The Black Jacobins* (1938), C.L.R. James wrote:

66 The struggle lasted for 12 years. The slaves defeated in turn the local whites and the soldiers of the French monarchy, a Spanish invasion, a British expedition of some 60,000 men, and a French expedition of similar size under Bonaparte's brother-in-law. [This] resulted in the establishment of the Negro state of Haiti which has lasted to this day. 99

In Britain feelings were mixed 'after San Domingo'. The poet Wordsworth wrote a sonnet *To Toussaint Louverture*. Others had more sympathy for the whites in the remaining colonies, who called for even tougher slave laws.

Why choose blacks?

The Spaniards who colonised Hispaniola in 1493 forced the native Arawaks to work for them for 20 years. This cut the Arawak population from over 600,000 to only 60,000. The Spaniards wanted another supply of labour. They decided to take blacks from the coast of Guinea for several reasons:

- Early sailors liked to keep their ships near to coasts as long as possible. Guinea was a convenient place to stop en route from Europe to the West Indies. Not until 1838, using different ships, would Indian labourers be shipped from Calcutta to the Caribbean.

- The seemingly endless pool of blacks in Africa did not enjoy the protection of a powerful state. Unskilled in modern warfare, they had no guns and were easy prey.

- Many Africans possessed skills that were very useful to the colonists. Some were great craftsmen with wood or metal, others had what was needed most of all in the new colonies – communal farming skills. Also, Africans were used to working in a hot climate. The Portuguese knew this, having already forced Africans to work on sugar plantations in Sao Tome.

- Finally, as the Trinidadian statesman, Eric Williams, has explained, the Africans' colour could be used against them. On islands where only whites were free, a dark skin served as a permanent prison uniform, an ever visible badge that said: 'I am a slave'. It was also used as an excuse for treating black workers differently from white servants, more like oxen or work-horses. Little wonder that some blacks came to hate the colour of their own skin.

Why slaves?

Why did the settlers want slaves at all, rather than paid workers? Because, as the governor of Barbados pointed out in 1676, it was possible to forced three unwilling slaves to work 'better and cheaper than one white man'. They could be forced to toil for longer hours, so planters got rich more quickly. The economist Charles Davenant calculated that the labour of one slave was worth 'six times as much as the labour of an Englishman at home'. Also, some slaves even gave birth to fresh slaves, who cost the planters nothing! The laws of the colonies said any baby born to a slave became a slave, too, the 'property' of the mother's 'owner'. Even if a baby's father was white, the child was not free – unless the slaveholder said so.

As blacks and whites were forbidden to marry (in British colonies at least), some planters were embarrassed when a pale-skinned slave or 'mulatto' was born on their estate. They quickly sent the new child far away, perhaps to England. But not all slaveholders were alike. Some mulattos were allowed to grow up with their mothers and were treated as favourites, with nobody saying openly who the father was. Many a planter kept silent until he died, then in his will set a slave free. This was disapproved of by other slaveholders.

This is from the will of John Brown Mitchell, a slaveholder in Jamaica who died in 1824. In it he leaves £200 to Mary Mitchell, 'my reputed child of colour'. He also leaves some money to buy the freedom of 'my reputed daughter Matilda Mitchell' who was a slave on a different estate in Jamaica.

17

The white Queen

Sir Walter Raleigh, who had attempted to found England's first colony in America in 1585, was one of many to have a black servant. Britain's black community was growing. Dramatic evidence of this is to be found in Elizabeth I's outburst of 1596:

66 Whereas the Queen's majesty . . . is highly discontented to understande the great number of negars and Blackamoores which (as she is informed) are crepte into this realm . . . as also for that the moste of them are infidels having no understanding of Christe or his Gospel: hath given especial commandment that the said kinde of people shall be with all speed avoided [banished] and discharged out of this her majesty's dominions . . . 99

The Queen's call met no response, and in 1601 she repeated it: again in vain. Black people were a part of the nation and here to stay.

Why was Elizabeth so unhappy to see black people living in her country? Was her concern that these blacks were poor and might add to the unrest in her realm, perhaps by joining up with discontented Catholics? There is no evidence that there were enough blacks here for her to be so alarmed.

We know that the Elizabethans attached great meaning to symbols and colours, and white had more positive associations than black. It is possible that Elizabeth was simply colour-prejudiced, like the characters in the tragedy of *Othello*, which Shakespeare had written by 1602.

There is another possibility. Were these threats to the 'infidels' a clever plan by the Queen to take the white majority's minds off the problems they faced? The danger of war was present throughout Elizabeth's reign; there were several outbreaks of plague; and of the last seven harvests in the sixteenth century, five failed, pushing up food prices to new heights.

Slaves for Christians?

Even if the first Elizabethans were prejudiced, how could they tolerate slavery? Part of the answer is that in Tudor Britain, and for the next few hundred years, there was much cruelty in society at all levels. Amongst the poor, bear-baiting and cock-fighting were popular. Those with more power were often cruel to people. Priests of the 'wrong' faith were burned alive or hung, drawn and quartered. Elizabeth I's father, Henry VIII, executed her mother, Anne Boleyn; Elizabeth herself had her niece executed. Up to 1712, women were executed for 'witchcraft'. Some West Indian planters bribed judges in England to give convicted prisoners a choice: the gallows or time as a servant on a plantation. (Few whites, though, were slaves as long as blacks. Some soon became overseers. Henry Morgan, a Welshman who was forced to work on a sugar estate in Barbados, became a privateer and then Governor of Jamaica before he was 30.)

Why did the Church not do anything to stop the cruelty of slavery?

Firstly, if someone like John Hawkins was a Christian, most Africans at that time were not. Brutality to heathens was tolerated – by Protestant England as much as by Catholics abroad.

Secondly, the slavers returned to port with stories to ease the consciences of whites at home. These Guinea blacks, the seamen said, were hardly human; they were more like certain apes whose existence was just being made known to Europe. If they were like animals, why not treat them as such?

It was also claimed that, since some Africans sold fellow-Africans into slavery, this proved how primitive they were. (But no-one thought to compare this with the cruelty common in Britain at the time!)

The sun-tanned look that is fashionable today was not sought after in Tudor times. Elizabeth I, who lived from 1533 to 1603, was usually portrayed as quite unnaturally white: 'without shadow', one historian said.

The myth that blacks were inferior beings lived on. It was so useful. Converting to Christianity did not help blacks much, because there were other myths: that, despite all the evidence to the contrary, most slaves were happy, or that God had meant blacks to be slaves.

Finally, before the machine age, vast profits were to be made by using unpaid workers. Many Christians soon owned plantations and burned their own distinctive brand into each slave's skin with a red-hot iron. Up to 1732 on the Codrington estate in Barbados, run by the Society for the Propagation of the Christian Gospel, new slaves were branded with the word: SOCIETY. As for the USA, where whites in the southern states kept slaves until 1865, Sir Winston Churchill wrote:

> 66 It was said that over six hundred and sixty thousand slaves were held by ministers of the Gospel and members of the different Protestant Churches. Thus the institution of slavery was not only defended by every argument of self-interest, but many a Southern pulpit championed it as a system ordained by the Creator and sanctified by the Gospel of Christ. 99

Azariah Pinney was sentenced to a year on the island of Nevis for his part in the Monmouth Rebellion (1685). He eventually became a planter. John Pinney inherited his Uncle Azariah's sugar plantations and became a planter, too. In a letter to England in 1765 he wrote:
'I've purchased nine Negroe slaves at St Kitts and can assure you I was shock'd at the first appearance of human flesh expos'd for sale. But surely God ordain'd 'em for the use and benefit of us: otherwise his Divine Will would have been made manifest by some particular sign or token.'

Who profited?

It was not only the owners of the big plantations, the 'plantocracy', who profited from the slave trade and from what slaves produced. For more then 200 years, thousands of British sailors were kept in work by the slave trade. A report to Parliament in 1788 found Birmingham had over 4,000 gun-makers, with 100,000 guns a year going to slave-traders. Textiles from Lancashire and Yorkshire were bought by slave-captains to barter with. Branding-irons were made by metal workers. Bristol and Liverpool became major ports through fitting out slave-ships and handling the cargoes they brought back. Between 1700 and the census of 1801, Bristol's population trebled and Liverpool's population soared from 5,000 to 78,000.

Banks and finance houses grew rich from the fees and interest they earned from merchants who borrowed money for their long voyages. Those who financed slaving expeditions and ran plantations with slaves included MPs and Mayors of London, Liverpool and Bristol, as well as families such as Baring and Barclay, names still famous in financial circles today.

Industrial plants were built to refine the imported raw sugar. Glassware was needed to bottle the rum. From about 1724 tropical timber was imported from the colonies, too, such as satinwood and mahogany from Jamaica. Because it was far less vulnerable to

Left: The carved heads of elephants and black Africans high on Liverpool's town hall are a reminder of the 'African trade' that made the city so rich.

In 1783 John Pinney retired from his plantations and became a sugar merchant in Bristol. In this fine Georgian House, which he had built in 1789, and which is now a museum, he frequently entertained William Wordsworth as well as Coleridge and Southey. His son Charles was Mayor of Bristol during the riots in 1831 (see page 35).

A desk in Adam style (mahogany and oak, veneered with rosewood and satinwood) made for Harewood House in about 1770, probably by Thomas Chippendale.

woodworm than walnut and harder than beechwood, this mahogany gave furniture-makers in Britain, like Chippendale, Hepplewhite and Sheraton, the means to develop new styles. At a simpler level, craftsmen made pipes for those newly addicted to tobacco.

Between 1750 and 1780 about 70 per cent of the government's total income came from taxes on goods from its colonies.

In addition, when planters retired to Britain with their fortunes, they created jobs here. They had grand country houses built and commissioned fine furniture and portraits for them. In the words of the Earl of Shelburne, speaking in a debate in the House of Lords in 1778:

66 ... there was scarce a space of ten miles together, throughout this country, where the house and estate of a rich West Indian were not to be seen. 99

People in Britain were not alone in seeking the goods that slaves produced. All Europe was eager to smoke tobacco, to buy goods made of cotton and to add sugar to food and newly-imported drinks (coffee, tea, cocoa, chocolate and rum).

Family Fortunes

As people saw the extravagant spending on houses, banquets and every kind of finery, a new saying sprang up: 'as rich as a West Indian'.

Some 'West Indians' used their money and influence to enter the nobility or to become MPs. In Parliament they could stop attempts to make slavery illegal. Others invested part of their wealth in new ideas, new machines or cotton mills. James Watt's work on the steam engine was carried on with the aid of West Indian finance. Ironworks were developed at Merthyr Tydfil with the profits made from supplying slaves in the 1770s. However unwillingly, the slaves in the colonies played a key role in the Industrial Revolution and also helped to secure the fortunes of families that were soon to dominate Britain's affairs. The first Lord Liverpool chose his title in memory of profits from the 'Africa trade' via that port; his son became Prime Minister in 1812. John Gladstone was a Liverpool businessman who invested in shipping, sugar, cotton and slavery in British Guiana and Jamaica. His accounts show that his fortune rose from £15,900 in 1795 to £40,700 in 1799, then £333,600 in 1820 and £520,550 in 1828. He was an MP from 1818 to 1827 and became a baronet. His son William was elected to Parliament at the age of 23 and went on to be Prime Minister three times (see page 35).

The British historian C. Hill said in 1989:

66 (Slavery) was the corner-stone of our eighteenth century predominance. The profits of the slave trade, and of slavery, contributed greatly to the accumulation of capital which made Britain the country of the first Industrial Revolution, and so consolidated her position as the greatest world power. 99

Harewood House, near Leeds. It was built in the 1770s for Edwin Lascelles, 1st Lord Harewood, who made a fortune in the West Indies. Robert Adam designed the interiors, Thomas Chippendale made the furniture and Joshua Reynolds painted portraits. The grounds were landscaped by 'Capability' Brown.

I own I am shocked at the purchase of slaves,
And fear those who buy them and sell them are knaves;
What I hear of their hardships, their tortures and groans
Is almost enough to draw pity from stones.
I pity them greatly, but I must be mum.
For how could we do without sugar and rum?
William Cowper, *Pity for poor Africans* 1788

4 In ships to Britain

Accessories

The number of Britain's colonies in the Caribbean grew throughout the seventeenth century, then again during the reign of George III (1760–1820). More ships sailed via Africa to the Caribbean and the size of Britain's Afro-Caribbean population grew. This received a fresh boost whenever the captain of a 'Guineaman' docked in his home port with a young black aboard: as a cabin boy, as a servant or as a gift to a patron.

Among the famous whites whom blacks served in the seventeenth century were Charles I, Charles II and Samuel Pepys, whose Diary noted on 5 April 1669:

“ For a cookmaid we have, ever since Bridget went, used a black-moore of Mr. Batalier's, (Doll), who dresses our meat mighty well, and we mightily pleased with her. **”**

In the eighteenth century it became the height of fashion for the rich to have an 'exotic' footman or page. Tagged in many cases with a metal collar which they were never allowed to remove, these black youngsters were not required to toil in the fields. They were a status symbol, used by society ladies as a fashion accessory to set off their own white-powdered charms. Young blacks were preferred: they were easier to handle. As they got older, they often ran away.

One eighteenth century account tells how the Verney family of Claydon House in Buckinghamshire had a coach-and-six that was escorted round the country by 'a brace of tall negroes, with silver French horns . . . bloweing very joyfully to behold and see'. There is also a story that when Claydon's two black trumpeters sounded reveille they would be answered by two others from the neighbouring property at Hillesden.

When the Earl of Sandwich returned from Portugal in 1662 in his ship, the *Royal James*, Samuel Pepys' diary for 30 May recorded what he had brought back with him: ' a little Turke and a negro, which are entended for [intended to be] pages to the two young ladies. Many birds and other pretty noveltys'.

This portrait in the National Portrait Gallery, London, is of Louise de Kéroualle, Duchess of Portsmouth. She was Charles II's favourite mistress. Her black companion in the portrait is not named.

At the quayside in Bristol, 1726.

The grave of Scipio Africanus, at Henbury, near Bristol. The epitaph on the headstone reads:
HERE
Lieth the Body of
SCIPIO AFRICANUS
Negro Servant to ye Right Honourable Charles William Earl of Suffolk and Bradon who died ye 21st December 1720 Aged 18 Years

This poem is engraved on the footstone of Scipio's grave.

Anna Maria was the daughter of Olaudah Equiano (see page 27).

I who was Born a PAGAN and a SLAVE
Now Sweetly Sleep a CHRISTIAN in my GRAVE
What tho' my hue was dark my SAVIOR's sight
Shall Change this darkness into radiant light
Such grace to me my lord on earth has given
To recommend me to my Lord in heaven
Whose glorious second coming here I wait
With saints and Angels Him to celebrate.

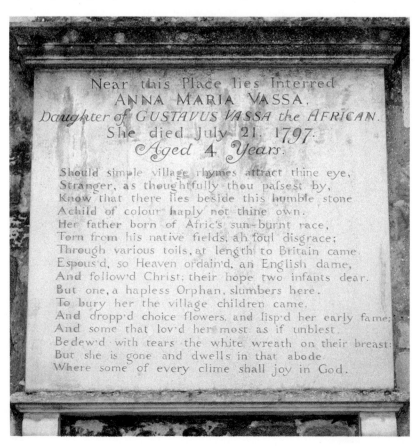

Epitaphs

If you go to St George's in Bermuda, you can see the gravestones of anonymous slaves buried outside the wall around the old Anglican churchyard. Here, the lack of epitaphs tells its own story.

If you go to the neatly-tended cemetery just outside Bristol, where young Scipio Africanus lies, you can read the text shown on the left. It seems that despite his black skin Scipio will be accepted in Heaven and he will be eternally grateful. His relationship to his 'owner' looks to be eternal, too. Perhaps it was the Earl himself who wrote the text!

The text about little Anna Maria Vassa (see below) is carved into a stone slab that hangs on the wall of St Andrew's church, Chesterton, on the fringe of Cambridge. It hangs very near the main door into the church. Like a constant sermon to those passing by, the epitaph uses the dead girl's colour to stress the all-loving nature of the Christian God.

Epitaphs, as well as telling us about the dead, often give us clues to the thoughts of the mourners. An epitaph to an Ethiopian slave, erected in the third century by the fair-skinned Greek who 'owned' him, says: 'his sun-baked skin may have been black, but his spirit was a bower of white blossoms'. Was it just by chance that the Greek spoke of *white* blossoms and not any other colour?

In the age of the British Empire, a soldier in a poem by Kipling praises an Indian bhisti (water-carrier) whose name is Gunga Din:

❝ An' for all 'is dirty 'ide
'E was white, clear white inside
When 'e went to tend the wounded under fire! ❞

Is it likely that the bhisti's insides were really white? Or does the British soldier, like the Greek before him, just see his own skin colour as a symbol for the highest quality, the best?

How free?

Right up to the late eighteenth century most black servants in Britain were clearly treated as the property of their masters and mistresses, just as slaves were in the colonies. Some blacks began to ask whether laws that were meant for the colonies were actually valid in Britain? If blacks ran away here, could they be legally reclaimed? Or might they turn to a court to protect them, just as any white could?

It seemed that no Parliament had ever passed a law about slavery on British soil. Decisions depended upon the attitude of the judge who was trying each case. For example, in 1694 a court ruled that 'heathens' could be treated as property and sold.

But what if runaways were baptised? In 1729 Sir Charles Talbot, the Solicitor-General, and Sir Phillip Yorke, the Attorney-General, held that this made no difference. Twenty years later, as Lord Chancellor, Yorke again clarified his view: '(a Negro slave) is as much property as any other thing'. But in 1762 the next Lord Chancellor contradicted this. Whose interpretation of the law was to be relied on?

For a very long time, all the judges in Britain were whites. (Even by 1989 there was only one black judge.) Could runaways trust a white judge to give them a fair hearing? With the stakes so high, it was risky for blacks to put their trust in anybody but themselves. A boy who served the Duchess of Kingston from the age of five or six became a handful in his teens, and was promptly shipped from London to the West Indies as a slave. 'Servants' who wanted to be sure of avoiding this fate did not wait for justice – they ran. The lucky ones disappeared

We are of Opinion, that a Slave by coming from the *West-Indies* to *Great Britain* or *Ireland*, either with or without his master, doth not become free, and that his Master's Property or Right in him is not thereby determined or varied: And that Baptism doth not bestow freedom on him, nor make any Alteration in his Temporal Condition in these Kingdoms. We are also of Opinion, that his Master may legally compel him to return again to the Plantations.
Jan. 14. 1729.   P. York.
                                             C. Talbot.

among the growing black communities in the dockland areas of the main ports. Just how often they ran may be judged from the frequent small advertisements offering rewards for their re-capture. These appeared just as soon as Britain had newspapers to carry them!

The legal opinion of two senior judges. Talbot was Lord Chancellor from 1733 to 1737 and Yorke (as Lord Hardwicke) from 1737 to 1756.

A variety of trades

Not all of the Afro-Caribbeans arriving in Britain in the eighteenth century came as cargo. Many were free blacks, ex-slaves who had been granted their freedom or had seized it. Many had taken their chance to escape during the American Revolution. In 1778, Thomas Jefferson estimated, more than 30,000 slaves ran from Virginia alone. Tens of thousands joined the British troops and were rewarded with their freedom. A 'Royal Ethiopian Regiment' was formed. When Britain lost the War, some of these 'Loyalists' settled in Canada or the Caribbean, but hundreds sailed to Britain with the returning troops.

Free black communities existed now in most ports that traded with the West Indies, and some of the men became seamen. Black people settled inland, too, if work was there. Black women sometimes worked as seamstresses or laundrymaids. The Duchess of Queensberry's servant Soubise, brought from St Kitts, was a fencing-master. One black servant, called Jarbé, could speak several languages and found work with the famous Italian socialite, Giovanni Casanova, who came to London in 1763. In London certain trades were not open to blacks because the Mayor in 1731 had barred blacks from serving apprenticeships. Many free blacks had no homes or jobs; and old records of fines and punishments show that many turned to begging.

Records show 'free' black citizens working in a wide range of jobs. Yet one thing linked them. For as long as slavery was legal, none of them was truly free.

Left: The family of Sir William Young with 'a Negro page', painted by J. Zoffany c. 1766 (detail).

Some blacks were on the streets during the Gordon Riots (1780), but Ignatius Sancho was not among them. He stayed inside his shop and watched.

A London shopkeeper

Ignatius Sancho (1729–1780) was born in mid-Atlantic on a slave-ship bound for Grenada. He was soon orphaned; his mother died and his father killed himself rather than be a slave. Sancho was sent to London at the age of two, and was named by his mistresses after a servant in a Spanish novel. He was kept from learning to read or write (these ladies believed that ignorance was 'the best and only' guarantee for obedience). Later, with encouragement from the Duke of Montagu, whose butler he became, Sancho taught himself.

He remained a servant until 1773, then married a woman from the West Indies, called Anne. They ran a grocer's shop which their son later turned into a bookseller's.

Ignatius Sancho knew many people in theatrical and literary circles, for example, Garrick, the actor, Lawrence Sterne and Dr Johnson. In 1768, his portrait was painted by Gainsborough. Sancho wrote, too, and his *Letters*, published in 1788 after his death, became a best-seller. One reviewer declared:

66 Let it no longer be said that Negers, as they are vulgarly called, are inferior to any white nation in mental abilities. 99

In the *Letters* Sancho was often critical, for example: 'The grand object of English navigators – indeed of all Christian navigators – is money, money money'.

Shortly before his death, Sancho saw the Gordon Riots, in which 300 people were killed and many buildings were destroyed. Watching this violence, by Protestants opposed to new rights for Catholics, he wondered whether whites in Britain would ever be ready to admit blacks into 'the fellowship of Christians'.

A gardener in Wales

'Jack Black' was kidnapped as a boy of eight from under his mother's eyes in the forests of Africa, where he was fishing. He was taken to a big estate at Ystumllyn in North Wales, and he was christened 'John Ystumllyn'. The memoirs of the grandson of the local doctor, written in Welsh, record that

66 John developed into a virile and agile young man, who learned both English and Welsh. The local damsels admired him, and competed for his attentions. He was married at Dolgellau Church around 1768. His wife's name was Margaret Griffith. They were blessed with seven children. One of his sons was employed as a game-keeper, a position he held until his death in 1862 at the age of 92 years. It is claimed that John was a quiet and kindly person, extremely skilful and a keen florist. His wife died in 1828 aged 81 years. 99

Could John Ystumllyn have found a black bride if he had wanted to? Probably not. The same was true for most other black men living in Britain before the 1950s. There were simply far fewer black women in Britain than there were black men. If John wanted to marry at all, he had little choice but to marry a white (and probably a poor woman with no title or dowry). His sons would face the same choice, no matter if this led to keen rivalry with white youths.

Constant inter-marriage meant that later generations were less visibly of African descent. This is one reason why the total number of black people in Britain remained low. At any given date before the twentieth century, Britain's black population was probably no more than 20–30,000.

The situation is different today. In recent times the balance of males and females in Britain's Afro-Caribbean population has become more even. It is easier for blacks to find black partners if they so choose. According to a 1976 survey of married 'West Indians' in Britain, only 8 per cent of men and 1 per cent of women had married a white partner. There are even dating agencies now, in big cities such as London, which specialise in introducing blacks to each other.

A portrait of John Ystumllyn, 1754.

According to the registers, John died in 1786, although the headstone of his grave states that he died, aged 46, in 1791. He is buried in a remote and beautiful churchyard amid green hills on which sheep graze.

THE COLOUR RIOTS.
REASONS FOR THE REPATRIATION.
TO THE EDITOR OF THE TIMES.

Sir,—May I, who have governed and served in West Indian Colonies for a long period of years, be permitted to say a word as to the present colour riots, which are likely to have a disastrous result?

It is an undeniable fact that, to almost every white man and woman who has lived a life among coloured races, intimate association between black or coloured men and white women is a thing of horror. And yet this feeling in no sense springs from hatred between the races. Every one of us has, probably, many faithful friends among the coloured people, whom we bear in our kindliest rememberence. It does not, either, I think, arise from any feeling of social superiority. The cause is far deeper. It is an instinctive certainty that sexual relations between white women and coloured men revolt our very nature.

Yours faithfully,
RALPH WILLIAMS.
St. James's Club, London, June 12.

COLOUR PREJUDICE
TO THE EDITOR OF THE TIMES.

Sir,—My attention has been drawn to a letter appearing in your issue of the 14th inst. over the signature of Sir Ralph Williams.

Sir Ralph expresses the view that intimate association between black men and white women is a thing of horror. Would it surprise Sir Ralph Williams to know that there are in South Africa 600,000 half-castes and that a similar number with a like parentage are to be found scattered over the various West India islands? Are we to take it then that Sir Ralph's fine sense of honour and delicacy is not shocked at the intimate immoral associations between white men and black women? Speaking myself as a man of colour, I might say that I am voicing the feelings of my own race when I declare that my whole mind revolts against the seduction of my women and girls by white men—young girls of 13 and 14 years of age are used to gratify that base lust of white seducers and are left with half-caste children on their hands to mourn the "honour" of the civilized white man.

I am, Sir, your obedient servant,
F. E. M. HERCULES, General Secretary, Society of Peoples of African Origin and Editor of the African Telegraph.
Lincoln House, High Holborn, WC1. June 16.

A former governor of the Windward Islands, Sir Ralph Williams, wrote on the subject of inter-marriage in a letter to *The Times* 14 June 1919 (far left). On 19 June 1919 there was a sharp reply by Felix Hercules, who had grown up in Trinidad and now lived in London (left).

25

Dido and Lady Elizabeth, two of Lord Mansfield's nieces.

Francis Barber, painted (probably) by Joshua Reynolds.

Dido Lindsay

A mulatto girl with the queenly name of Dido lived in the household of Lord Mansfield, who was Chief Justice from 1756 to 1788. A visitor noted in 1779 that Dido was treated with some fondness. The same visitor was told that the judge's nephew, Sir John Lindsay, 'having taken her mother prisoner in a Spanish vessel, brought her to England, where she was delivered of this girl'.

Dido supervised the family estate's dairy and poultry yard. In a will dated 1783, Earl Mansfield left her £500 plus £100 a year for life and stated that she was free. Five years later the judge's nephew died. It was only then, from his obituary notice, that it became clear exactly who Dido was: namely, Sir John's illegitimate daughter.

A Midlands schoolteacher

Francis Barber (1735?–1801) was brought from Jamaica to Yorkshire as a boy and set free in the final will of his 'owner'. For the next thirty years, apart from when he ran away to sea, Barber was a servant to Dr Samuel Johnson, who paid fees of £300 for Barber to be educated at a grammar school from 1767 to 1772. On Johnson's death in 1784, Barber opened a school himself, at Burntwood near Lichfield, which he ran with the help of his wife, Elizabeth. Their son became a Methodist preacher.

James Boswell, Johnson's companion and biographer, thought Johnson was far too kind to Barber. Boswell was full of prejudice and believed that Africans were better off as slaves than left in their own land. On a journey to the Hebrides in 1773, he met Gory, a black servant who had been baptised by the Bishop of Durham. Boswell felt it odd 'to see an African in the north of Scotland, with little or no difference of manners from those of the natives'.

Johnson, by contrast, had a horror of slavery and the blind pursuit of riches. He knew, too, how hard the slaves were fighting to free themselves. Once, during a visit to Oxford, he drank a toast 'to the next insurrection of the Negroes in the West Indies'.

5 Stirring consciences

'Books upon a shelf'

Ukawsaw Gronniosaw

Robinson Crusoe, published in 1719, gave a white man's view of blacks. Eventually, in 1770, the tables were turned, when the memoirs of a black man were published.

This amazing autobiography told how Ukawsaw Gronniosaw was sold to a slaver for two yards of cloth. He was taken to Barbados, then resold to a clergyman, who sent him to school and eventually set him free. After serving with the British Army in the Caribbean, Gronniosaw came to London. He married a white woman, a widowed weaver called Betty, who had a child to look after. They scraped a living in East Anglia and the Midlands. The descriptions of whites' behaviour towards them, both good and bad, are a key feature of the narrative.

This moving story was circulated with the hope of influencing public opinion, and more blacks were urged to write about their lives. Some whites, however, would only believe what a white man told them. This is where somebody like the Reverend John Newton was useful.

Before he became a priest, Newton had been captain of a slave-ship. Speaking from personal experience, he described how the slaves he supplied to Antigua seldom lived more than nine years. Planters there found it cheaper to work their slaves to death and then replace them, than to improve their working conditions. Newton was also able to bring home most vividly how kidnapped blacks suffered during the middle passage! They were forced 'to lie in two rows, one above the other, on each side of the ship, close to each other like books upon a shelf' (see page 12).

Olaudah Equiano (1745–97)

The most fascinating autobiography to appear in the eighteenth century was that of Olaudah Equiano. In an age when many people never left their home county all their lives, Equiano's fortunes and misfortunes took him from the interior of West Africa – where he was kidnapped as a boy of ten – to the Caribbean, the USA, Canada and Europe, and even to the Arctic. He saw snakes in Central America, camel trains in Turkey, and whales, walruses and polar bears north of Spitzbergen. He was forced into slavery in Barbados, resold north to Virginia, brought to England in 1757 and resold to the West Indies five years later. He was often lonely. He had been captured together with his sister, but they were separated and he never saw any of his family again. His various masters ignored his original Ibo name and called him Michael or Jacob or Gustavus Vassa. Eventually, through countless little dealings he was able to get the £40 together he needed to buy his freedom. Equiano went on to work on merchant ships and Royal Navy vessels. He felled mahogany in Nicaragua and even became a hairdresser.

In 1768 two black servants had sailed on James Cook's first voyage. In 1773 Equiano went one better, sailing as a doctor's assistant on an expedition in which Horatio Nelson took part. Led by Captain Phipps, they were looking for a new route to India and, before having to

Olaudah Equiano, also known as Gustavus Vassa.

In the Arctic

'On 20 June [1773] we began to use Dr Irving's apparatus for making salt-water fresh. I used to attend the distillery. I frequently purified from twenty-six to forty gallons a day (...). On 28 June, being in lat. 78°, we made Greenland, where I was surprised to see the sun did not set (...) and on the 27th [July] we got as far north as 80°37'; and in 19 or 20 degrees east longitude from London. On 29 and 30 July we saw one continued plain of smooth unbroken ice, bounded only by the horizon. We remained hereabouts until 1 August, when the two ships got completely fastened in the ice, occasioned by the loose ice that set in from the sea. This made our situation very dreadful and alarming, so that on the seventh day we were in very great apprehension of having the ships squeezed to pieces. The officers now held a council to know what was best for us to do in order to save our lives, and determined that we should endeavour to escape by dragging our boats [life-boats] along the ice towards the sea, which, however, was farther off than any of us thought. While we were at this hard labour I once fell into a pond we had made amongst some loose ice and was very near being drowned. It was the eleventh day of the ships being fastened, and the fourth of our drawing the boats in this manner, that the wind changed to the E.N.E. The weather immediately became mild and the ice broke towards the sea.'

From the autobiography of Olaudah Equiano

Trapped in the Arctic ice!

give up, reached a more northerly point than any ship from Europe before them.

Equiano toured England, Scotland and Ireland in an effort to win support against slavery from white people. The huge success of his autobiography, published in 1789, aided his campaign. It was reprinted seventeen times and it was translated into several foreign languages.

On 7 April 1792, he married Susan Cullen at Soham in Cambridgshire. Sadly he died only five years later. One of his two daughters, Joanna, was still alive in 1816. Cambridgeshire records show that she inherited her father's legacy of £950 when she turned twenty-one. His first-born daughter, Anna Maria, did not survive him so long (see page 22).

This slogan was used frequently in the campaign against slavery.

Free to go

Whites' consciences had slept for 200 years, but there was an awakening in the second half of the eighteenth century. Quakers stirred first. Some who were slaveholders freed their slaves. Methodists and Baptists, too, petitioned Parliament. In *Thoughts on Slavery*, 1774, John Wesley, the Methodist leader, called upon every slaveholder and on God:

&& O burst thou all their chains in sunder. 99

At the same time as this support was growing, blacks were faced with new attacks upon them. Some whites valued blacks as slaves in the colonies, but they did not want to see blacks in Britain, especially not any who were free.

In *The Gentleman's Magazine* in 1764 a writer complained that there were 20,000 blacks in London alone. A judge, Sir John Fielding, complained in 1768 that free blacks were always at the quayside 'to corrupt and dissatisfy the Mind of every fresh black Servant that comes to England'. And there was no limit to the solidarity these free blacks showed towards those not yet free. They wrote autobiographical narratives and some dared to write stinging pamphlets or letters to the press. (Such writers included Sancho, Equiano and Ottobah Cugoano, who arrived in London in 1772 after being a slave in Grenada.)

Some blacks, seen by whites as a nuisance, were beggars such as disabled ex-servicemen, who now relied on charity. After a severe winter in 1785–86, when many blacks and whites had joined queues for food hand-outs, a Government scheme was devised to create a settlement for free blacks near the River Rokel in what is now known as Sierra Leone in West Africa. Convicts had long been transported to the colonies, so why not ship blacks to Africa? In the words of the minister responsible, Lord Sydney:

> 66 (it is a plan) for sending out of this Country a Number of Black Poor (many of whom have been discharged from His Majesty's Naval Service at the Conclusion of the late War, and others after having been employed with the Army in North America) who have since their Arrival in England been reduced to the greatest Distress. Measures should immediately be taken for acquiring from the Native Chiefs a Territory of sufficient Extent for the settling of the said Black Poor, and also for furnishing them with Tools and Implements. 99

Free to stay?

Equiano was asked to help organise the venture. But few blacks were keen. Ottobah Cugoano, who often spoke up for the black community, explained why. To blacks born in the Caribbean or America, Africa was an unknown continent; too little money was being put into the scheme; the views of the 'Native Chiefs' were not known; slave-ships still preyed on that region. Very close to the chosen site, Cugoano observed, the British themselves still maintained 'forts and garrisons, to ensnare, merchandize, and to carry others into captivity and slavery'.

To encourage the 'said Black Poor' to sign up for Sierra Leone, new laws were enacted. Poor relief was now to go only to whites, and any blacks found begging were to be put on a ship by force, no matter what service they had given to Britain in the army or navy. Blacks who criticised these laws, or any details of the scheme, faced racial abuse in the *Morning Post* on 30 December 1786:

> 66 Are we to be told what plans should be adopted by a crew of reptiles, manifestly only a single link in the great chain of existence above the monkey? A few constables to disperse their meetings, and a law, prohibiting blacks from entering our country, would be the proper mode of treating those creatures, whose intercourse with the inferior orders of our women is disgraceful to the state. 99

'Am I not a woman and a sister?'

The 'Bridgtower sonata'

Evidently, the King and Queen, whilst firm supporters of colonial slavery, did not share the views of the *Morning Post*. For only three years later they invited a black to Windsor Castle. He was a lad of nine or ten, whose skill could be rivalled by few, black or white. His name was George Bridgtower (1779–1860) and he was acknowledged to be one of the finest violinists of his day. The boy had possibly been taught by Haydn (and his brother, too, who became a cellist). What is certain is that in 1803 George was invited to Vienna, where he gave the very first performance of Beethoven's *opus* 47 – with the composer himself at the piano.

From 1789 Bridgtower lived mostly in England and in 1811 he wrote some music that gained him the degree of Bachelor of Music at Cambridge. He was first violin in the Prince of Wales' own band for 14 years; but he appeared in Paris and other major cities, too. His father came from Barbados and served Prince Esterhazy in Austria, his mother was of German-Polish descent. They must have been proud when Beethoven dedicated *opus* 47 to George – and disappointed, surely, when after a tiff with George over a girl, Beethoven renamed the work: The 'Kreutzer Sonata'.

Starring as Wotan: Willard White.

Talented black musicians were heard in Britain in Tudor times, and today blacks dominate the pop charts. Everybody is familiar with the names of successful black musicians from the worlds of jazz, gospel, soul, reggae and other forms of popular music. Opera buffs, too, appreciate black singers, and not only in roles such as Carmen or Porgy – now even as Wagner's god Wotan, which was sung throughout Britain in 1989 by Willard White, a bass baritone born in Jamaica. Should it come as a surprise that blacks have a history of achievement in classical music?

6 Challenging the law

Numerous African-Americans have been commemorated on US postage stamps, among them Frederick Douglass (1817?–1895) and Harriet Tubman (1820?–1913). No black has been commemorated on a UK stamp.

Non-violent resistance

In Jamaica, in 1760, a young slave named Tacky led a violent uprising backed by tens of thousands of slaves. When news of this reached Britain, white opinion was divided. To some it proved the need, if blacks were so savage, for more cruel laws. Others realised that slaves must be less content than was often made out. But were they right to use force in attempting to break free? A pamphlet that circulated in London in 1760, under a pseudonym, saw no alternative:

66 And so all the black men in our plantations, who have none upon earth to appeal to, may lawfully repel that force with force, and to recover their liberty, destroy their oppressors; and it is the duty of others, white as well as blacks, to assist. 99

Later in the USA, in 1859, a former slave and a leading anti-slavery campaigner, Fredrick Douglass, was also unwilling to condemn any violence used in this cause:

In slave colonies in the Caribbean and in America's Deep South, where whites were a minority, blacks could try fighting their way to freedom – like Leonard Parkinson, shown here, a Jamaican maroon. However, blacks in Britain were in a different situation.

66 Let every man work for the abolition of Slavery in his own way. I would help all and hinder none. 99

Within Britain, however, the blacks were a minority. Their struggle had to take other forms. One thing they could and did do was run away. If they were not found, they were free. If they were found, but whites needed to go to court to reclaim their 'property', blacks had a chance to put their case. With the help of a lawyer, they could challenge the morality of laws that treated people as things. Blacks were human; and each time a judge was prepared to admit this, one runaway was set free – and freedom for all slaves came a step closer.

It was not easy for blacks to find a lawyer. All the lawyers were white men, trained to help property-owners. What could they gain by defending a runaway black? There was no large fee to be earned and they might annoy an influential person and damage their careers. One slaveholder, angry at losing his 'property', challenged the successful defence lawyer to a duel! Yet if a white's life was sometimes at risk in these cases, a black's always was. For example, when John Annis lost his appeal, he was at once shipped back to St Kitts and flogged mercilessly.

Fortunately, blacks who dared to run away did encounter a few whites with legal talent who were prepared to help. Equiano's friend, Granville Sharp, a grandson of the Archbishop of York, devoted two years to teaching himself law in order to be able to do so. The example set by those like Sharp, who went out of their way to challenge the powerful in defence of others' rights, is just one reason why 'black history' should be studied by whites, too.

Jonathan Strong

In 1740 Thomas Arne composed 'Rule Britannia', which declared that the people of Britain would never be slaves. Could that apply to blacks, too? In 1765, a youth called Jonathan Strong had to find out fast. Or else!

Jonathan had been pistol-whipped and left for dead in a London street by the man who had brought him from Barbados as a slave. He was spotted by Granville Sharp and taken to hospital. After four months he recovered sufficiently to take a job, and he was baptised.

However, two years laters he was recognised by his 'owner' – who had never formally set him free. To the youth's horror, this man now sold him to a planter about to sail for Jamaica, who quickly had him locked up until his ship sailed. The situation was desperate. Somehow Jonathan got word to Sharp, who hastily appealed to the courts. But what about Jonathan? The youth was taken before the Lord Mayor of London. Would he rule slavery illegal? – No. Would he at least grant Jonathan his liberty? – Yes! The captain of the planter's ship, quite unprepared for such a ruling, leapt up in court and grabbed the boy's arm. But in vain. Jonathan Strong walked free.

Later, more blacks in peril would turn for help to Granville Sharp, for judges would listen to a white more readily than to a black.

'Granville Sharp rescuing a slave from the hands of his master'

James Somerset

After two years in England, James Somerset escaped from his 'owner'. But he was recaptured and put in irons on the *Ann and Mary*, a ship bound for Jamaica. Thanks to Sharp, James went to court, where his case became famous. For he did not just demand his own freedom. There were 10–20,000 'servants' in Britain, it was said, and he sought a legal ruling that would set them all free. It was now November 1771, was it not time?

The case was tried by Lord Mansfield, the Lord Chief Justice, who was widely expected to support the right of the wealthy to keep their 'property'. But he had a black girl called Dido (see page 26) serving in his own household. Could she tilt the balance in James Somerset's favour? 'No doubt, he will be set free', one Jamaica planter said, 'for Lord Mansfield keeps a black in his house which governs him and the whole family' The case dragged on. It would have suited the judge if the matter could have been settled out of court, then he need not have made a ruling. But both parties refused to do this.

Finally, in June 1772, Lord Mansfield compromised. Noting that there was no law that positively permitted slavery in England or allowed slaves to be shipped out of England by force, he set James free. His judgement did not quite make slavery here illegal or mean 'servants' were entitled to wages. However, if people like Jonathan and James ran away now and their 'owners' tried to smuggle them aboard ships, they could rely on the law to defend them. Providing that help reached them before high tide . . .

What next?

After James Somerset's victory, more and more blacks in Britain gained their freedom. The main hold over them had gone. For slavery to end in the colonies, however, more than a court decision was needed. Laws did exist that allowed slavery overseas, and these had to be changed. How could that be done?

There was only one way. A majority of the Members of Parliament (white men, there were no black MPs then) would have to vote to repeal these laws. That was unlikely. In the eighteenth century MPs were elected only by men of property; over 300 MPs were simply nominated by rich landowners and dozens of 'West Indians', that is, white men who had made fortunes in the West Indies. They stood for privilege and hated any talk of radical change or 'rights'. Even MPs with no overseas interest were afraid that to abolish slavery could set a dangerous precedent. If the rich were to give up one kind of 'property', which would they be asked to give up next? 'Once adopt that principle and there was an end to all property,' one Member said.

George III, who reigned over a growing number of Caribbean colonies, and other members of the royal family opposed abolition. Indeed, as an honour, the freedom of Liverpool was granted to one of the King's sons for his speeches in the House of Lords in defence of the African slave trade. (This was the Duke of Clarence, who in 1830 was to become William IV.)

Lord North, who was Prime Minister from 1770 to 1782, defended slavery so as not to upset the white colonists in America – who might otherwise decide to seek independence from Britain. Later, when that happened anyway, he told Parliament that the slave trade could not be ended as it had become necessary to almost every nation in Europe!

Before a majority of MPs would oppose slavery, three things needed to happen:

- the King's influence had to become less
- other sources of income, greater than the profits from West Indian products, were needed
- lots of whites had to press for the election laws to be changed, so that non-wealthy MPs could be elected.

Changing views

It was not only wealthy whites who backed slavery. Poor whites could go to the West Indies as overseers and clerks and enjoy a status they could never achieve at home. Yet many ordinary whites did eventually call for slavery in the Caribbean to end. Why?

There was an awakening of interest in Christianity as practised by Quakers, Methodists and Baptists. Nonconformists could not

become MPs yet; so they could only appeal for new laws, not make them. But appeal they did. 1,900 petitions came just from Methodist congregations. Anglicans like Granville Sharp and James Ramsay joined them. Thomas Clarkson, a key member of the Society for the Abolition of Slavery, travelled 35,000 miles in seven years, gathering evidence on slavery and lecturing against it.

Working people were forming radical movements to demand more rights for themselves. Some spoke of revolution. It seemed natural to support blacks who wanted justice, too. Petitions flooded into Parliament, signed at first by tens of thousands. Later, one petition alone was signed by 350,000 women.

Some MPs, motivated by Christianity, responded to the petitions. They were not revolutionaries. Starting with a modest bill in 1788 to limit the number of slaves a ship could carry (according to its tonnage), they moved on to a bill to stop the supplying of new slaves from Africa. This was proposed by William Wilberforce, MP for Hull, a few weeks before the storming of the Bastille and the beginning of the French Revolution.

Not a revolution, but …

The 1789 bill was voted down. It was proposed again, year after year, and its chances grew. George III became less of a force because of recurring illness. Then, in the early nineteenth century, the West India lobby was split over two of the newest colonies: Trinidad and British Guiana. Those with estates there wanted more slaves; but planters in other parts of the Caribbean saw them as rivals and thought it better to limit the supply of new slaves.

There were MPs, too, who had their eyes on other parts of the globe. Britain was developing colonies in Ceylon, at Cape Horn and elsewhere. Thus, in 1807, the year the new East India Docks opened in London, a new bill was supported by the Foreign Secretary (the future Lord Grey) – and became law!

This painting of the 'Death of Nelson' in 1805 by C. W. Sharpe is an imaginative reconstruction. Was a black seaman really so close by? Certainly, like Gronniosaw and Wedderburn, black people have been part of Britain's armed forces for centuries.

The new law was limited. It did not end slavery within colonies, only the shipment of slaves to them. Yet it had teeth. The Navy was ordered to blockade Guinea and arrest slave-ships. Once the Navy had protected slavers from pirates, now it turned its cannons towards the slavers. Denmark had enacted a similar law in 1802. By 1820 the USA, France, Spain and Portugal had followed. Slave-ships still plied the Atlantic, but now as smugglers. It was a start.

Robert Wedderburn

Any veterans returning from the Napoleonic Wars in 1815 with hopes of a better world must have felt as frustrated as the mass of people working in the rising manufacturing towns. For, still, only property-owners were allowed to vote; and the Prime Minister of the day, Lord Liverpool, the son of a wealthy 'West Indian', could not be relied on to bring in new laws that would change the old order of things. So, with marches and rallies, huge numbers of people called for the reform of Parliament. Tens of thousands demonstrated, up and down the country, with shoemakers and weavers and blacks like the Reverend Robert Wedderburn marching with them.

Wedderburn was the son of a Scottish planter and a slave. He left Jamaica in 1778 and worked on a warship. Then he became a Unitarian preacher and from 1819 ran a chapel in Soho, where he blended fiery religion with radical politics. Missionaries who preached 'passive obedience' to slaves made him angry. He sent pamphlets to Jamaica, warning slave-holders that: 'the fate of St Domingo awaits you' (see page 16). In England he urged people to arm themselves ready for a revolution. He was accused of blasphemy and sent to jail for two years. He said:

66 As to my explanation of the doctrines of Christ ... He was like myself, one of the lower order, and a genuine radical reformer. Being poor himself, he knew how to feel for the poor, and despised the rich for the hardness of their hearts. His principles were purely republican; he told his followers they were all brethren and equals. 99

William Davidson

So long as Lord Liverpool was Prime Minister, from 1812 to 1827, the police or troops were used to suppress protest: at Spa Fields in London in 1816, for example, or during the march of the Blanketeers in 1817. The 'Peterloo massacre' took place in Manchester in 1819. Sixty thousand men, women and children had gathered in St Peter's Field to hear Henry 'Orator' Hunt speak. But a signal was given to disperse them and troops on horseback – sabres drawn – were sent slashing into the crowd. Eleven protestors were killed and over 400 wounded.

Hunt was arrested and later jailed. Then, to prevent future protests, the Government brought in 'Six Acts'. These banned public meetings of more than 50 people; allowed homes to be searched more readily; made practising the use of arms a crime; and imposed a new tax on pamphlets. With lawful protest stifled, only one response made sense to William Davidson, the son of Jamaica's white attorney-general and a slave, and that was revolt. Davidson joined four white men in the 'Cato Street conspiracy' – a desperate plot to assassinate the whole Cabinet, as a signal for a general uprising.

Can Davidson be compared with the Germans who laid a plot in 1944 to kill Hitler? Or was Davidson just a criminal? At Nuremberg, after World War II, the Allies said unjust laws need not be obeyed and tyrants should be opposed. But were the rulers of slave colonies tyrants? In one point, at least, both plots were alike: they failed. Davidson and his friends were betrayed by a police spy – who worked out the details of the plot for them and then led them into a trap! All five men were publicly hanged on 1 May 1820 and then beheaded.

The 'Peterloo Massacre', 1819.

Reasons for change

Revolts in the colonies

In 1823 a big revolt in British Guiana was led by Quamina Gladstone, a deacon, and his son Jacky. Both were slaves on the estate of Sir John Gladstone, MP. When it was over, Quamina's bullet-ridden body was put on show, to deter others.

On Sunday 25 December 1831, Christmas Day, tens of thousands in western Jamaica left their work and rose under the leadership of Samuel Sharpe, a Baptist deacon. During two weeks of fighting, 14 whites and 200 rebels were killed and property worth over a million pounds was destroyed. 312 rebels were then executed, including Samuel Sharpe himself, who said:

❝I would rather die on yonder gallows than live in slavery. ❞

Each new uprising in the West Indies stirred the consciences of more whites in Britain, especially if Christians were involved. Other whites worried more about the costs. For revolts not only damaged property, they kept troops away from other parts of the globe where Britain had interests.

New interests

In 1806, before the law to end the slave trade, the West Indies had taken 21 per cent of Britain's exports. By 1830 its share was less than 11 per cent. 'King Sugar' no longer ruled. Many things were more important to Britain's economy now. Since the Battle of Waterloo in 1815 the price of sugar had halved. Other places could supply it (such as Mauritius, a British colony since 1814). The USA and India provided far more cotton than the West Indies ever could. If slavery were abolished, only the slave-holders looked set to lose much. Britain's long involvement with slavery had given it the chance to become an economic and military giant. Mills and factories had sprung up. What the mills needed was customers to buy the goods they produced.

Oh me good friend, Mr Wilberforce, make we free!
God Almighty thank ye! God Almighty thank ye!
God Almighty make me free!
Buckra in this country no make me free!
What negro for to do? What negro for to do?
Take force with force! Take force with force!
     – a slave song from Jamaica, 1816

Moral presssure

Mary Prince was brought to Britain in 1828. Her 'owners' threatened to throw her out if she was not content with her situation, so she left them. She was at liberty now; but her husband was back in Barbados. If she tried to rejoin him there, would she be returning to a life of slavery? In 1831 she published *The History of Mary Prince, A West Indian Slave, Related by Herself*. In it, she made this appeal:

❝How can slaves be happy when they have the halter round their neck and the whip upon their back and are separated from their mothers, and husbands, and children, and sisters, just as cattle are sold and separated? I have often wondered how English people can go out to the West Indies and act in such a beastly manner. But when they go to the West Indies they forget God and all feeling of shame. I have been a slave myself – I know what slaves feel. The man that says that slaves be quite happy in slavery – and they do not want to be free – that man is either ignorant or a lying person. I never heard a slave say so. Liberty. That is what we want. We do not mind hard work, if we had proper treatment, and proper wages. But they will have work-work-work, night and day, sick and well, till we are quite done up. I tell it to let English people know the truth; and I hope they will never leave off to pray to God, and call loud to the great King of England, till all the poor blacks be given free, and slavery done up for evermore. ❞

Riots in Britain

The pressure to reform Parliament raged on. It came from abolitionists and from workers. It came from the mill-owners, too, who were Britain's new rich. They wanted a Government that would make laws to help them, not just the 'West Indian' MPs and other landowners.

In 1830, prompted partly by events in Paris, Britain's new king, William IV, feared serious unrest if some reforms were not made; so he chose Lord Grey as his Prime Minister. In 1831, Grey asked Parliament to allow more men to take part in elections, about 50 per cent more. When this was voted down, he called a general election. After the election, the King wanted the Duke of Wellington to be Prime Minister but he was forced to call on Grey

Rioting in Bristol, 1831

again. This time the bill was passed by the House of Commons, only to be defeated by the House of Lords. At this, riots broke out in several towns. The country was in turmoil. In Bristol, the town hall, the bishop's palace and the jails were set on fire. In Nottingham, the castle – home of a wealthy member of the House of Lords – was burned down. Grey asked the King to create an extra 50 lords to tip the balance in favour of his bill. His opponents were beaten. In June 1832, his Reform Act became law. Did a Parliament now exist that would vote to abolish slavery, too?

Threat of independence

Planters in the Caribbean, who were kept well informed of the changes going on in Britain, were increasingly worried that Parliament would free their slaves. They held meetings and discussed the idea of breaking away from British rule, perhaps by joining the USA, which still allowed slavery south of the Ohio River.

Not all Caribbean slaveholders actually lived in the Caribbean, however. Some of the biggest estates were owned by absentee landlords, such as the Earl of Harewood, who lived 8,000 kilometres away in Britain. They were in a different position from those on the spot. If the West Indies became independent, absentee landlords stood to lose greatly.

By August 1832 they wanted to negotiate with Grey's government. Their talks dragged on for almost a year. An MP called Marryat,

ABOLITION OF SLAVERY.] Mr. William C. Gladstone wished to allude to certain observations made by the noble Lord, the late Under-Secretary for the Colonies, in his speech to the House on Tuesday night. The noble Lord had selected an estate in Demerara, belonging to his [Gladstone's] nearest relative, for the purpose of showing what a destruction of human life had taken place in the West Indies, from the manner in which the slaves were worked. The noble Lord stated, that, in three years, a decrease of seventy-one slaves had taken place on the estate of Vreeden Hoop, which he attributed to the increased cultivation of sugar; but... he would ask, were there not certain employments in this and other countries more destructive to life than others? He would instance those of painting, and working in lead mines, both of which were well known to have that tendency. The noble Lord attempted to impugn the character of the gentleman acting as manger of his [Gladstone's] estates; and in making this selection, he had certainly been most unfortunate; for there was not an individual in the colony more proverbial for humanity, and the kind treatment of his slaves, than Mr. Maclean. He held in his hand two letters from Mr. Maclean, in which that gentleman spoke in the kindest terms of the people under his charge; described their state of happiness content, and healthiness; their good conduct, and the infrequency of severe punishment; and recommended certain additional comforts, which he said the slaves well deserved.

These records from the House of Commons show how, even as late as 17 May 1833, there were MPs ready to defend slaveholders and their managers. William Gladstone, of course, was himself the son of a slave holder (see opposite page and page 20). In his own personal diary Gladstone wrote: 'spoke for 50 min. My leading desire was to benefit the cause of those who are now so sorely beset. The House heard me very kindly, and my *friends* were satisfied. Tea afterwards at the Carlton.'

35

This is how F. Biard pictured the moment when the slaves in French colonies were freed on 27 April 1848.

In a letter from South America, dated 22 May 1833, Charles Darwin wrote:

'I have watched how steadily the general feeling, as shown at elections, has been rising against Slavery. What a proud thing for England if she is the first European nation which utterly abolishes it!'

who had been 'instructed on behalf of the colony of Grenada, whose interests he represented', summed up their position. They would free their slaves on certain conditions ...

Free at last!

In 1833, Parliament finally said slaves were to be freed. This was a moment in British history that both whites and blacks can celebrate. The details are more complicated. The new law did not take effect until 1 August 1834. Even then, only those aged under six were to be entirely free. To please the West India lobby, who would have voted against it, two 'sweeteners' had been written into the new law:

- The Government would pay compensation to the slaveholders: about £37 per slave freed, depending on age and sex. (The Gladstones, for example, freed 2,183 slaves in Jamaica and Guiana and received £85,606.)

- Slaves would now become 'apprentices', that is, they could be treated as if they had signed a contract to work unpaid for their former 'owners' for six years.

The law was a compromise. The Government was saved the expense of a military solution. But the slaveholders had wanted the unpaid apprenticeship scheme to run for 12 years. They were also unhappy that planters could now not make blacks work over 10 hours a day or 45 hours a week without paying them. And they had wanted higher compensation (although, in total, some £20 million was paid to them – almost as much as the Government's annual budget, which led William Cobbett to complain that this money was coming from Britain's 'tax-paying slaves'). As for the slaves, who were paid no compensation and told to go on working for the master in his fine house, their joy was mixed with anger. In St Kitts both men and women downed tools, and only brutality by the militia forced them back to work.

In some colonies the apprenticeship scheme was ignored and all slaves were simply freed. Everywhere else there was a clamour for the same. In the end, as a result of all the pressure, Parliament gave way and ended the scheme early. At midnight on 1 August 1838, freedom came at last. As thousands of black people gave thanks – at churches, chapels, public meetings and parades throughout the British West Indies – peals of bells rang out. Whites' fears of widespread acts of revenge were ill founded. The celebrations were peaceful, a mark of the character of the black community.

The Cayman Islands: a case history

Here are a few details from the history of one tiny Caribbean colony up to the emancipation (freeing) of slaves there.

Columbus was the first white man to notice the Cayman Islands, but the first English visitor was Francis Drake, after he had plundered Spanish settlements on Hispaniola. His log of 1586 refers to the 'islands of Caymanas'. Captain William Jackson's log of 1643 notes:

66 There be 2 Islands of ye same name, being by ye Spanyards called Chimanoe (crocodile). Hither doe infinnit numbers of sea tortoises resorte. The islands is much frequented by English, Dutch and French ships, that come purposely to salt up ye flesh of these Tortoises. 99

In 1655 Oliver Cromwell's army took Jamaica from the Spanish, and tradition has it that the first settlers in the Caymans were deserters from that army.

The Treaty of Madrid in 1670 gave to England all of the Spanish islands and colonies whatsoever in the West Indies. Spain retained colonies only on the mainland. The settlements on the Caymans still continued to be prey to Spanish privateers. Equally, in 1671 Henry Morgan (see page 18) watered his ship in the Caymans and sailed off to attack Spain's mainland colony of Panama, his loot totalling some six million crowns. After this, Charles II knighted Morgan and made him Governor of Jamaica and of the Caymans (which were linked by government until Jamaica's independence in 1962).

After the Treaty of Utrecht in 1713 (which gave Britain more colonies and a contract to supply 4,800 slaves per year to Spain's colonies) the Caymans became a popular lair for pirates, including noted cut-throats such as Edward Teach, better known as Blackbeard. More permanent settlers occur in records of 1734, when land was granted to arrivals from Britain. In 1742 Mary Bodden was granted 1,000 acres.

In 1774 the population was put at 176. A census of 1801 showed 933, of whom 551

were slaves. According to *The Cayman Islands Handbook* (1980):

66 Emancipation of slaves took place by proclamation on May 3, 1835, under an apprenticeship scheme. In 1837, the Governor of Jamaica, the Marquis of Sligo, discharged the remaining terms of apprenticeship. At the time there were 954 slaves in Grand Cayman, eight in Little Cayman, but apparently none in Cayman Brac. There [were] 116 slave owners. The largest number of slaves was owned by Mary Bodden of Bodden Town, who owned 45. Next came John Michael Webster, also of Bodden Town, who owned 39. These figures come from the return on slave ownership which was compiled in order that slave owners might be paid compensation. The return gives an interesting survey of principal families in the islands. Of the slave owning families 22 were Boddens, 13 were Watlers, ... 99

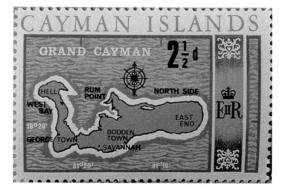

In 1991 the Cayman Islands were still a British colony. However, most of the 24,900 islanders now enjoyed a high standard of living – if no longer from farming. The Caymans had become a tax haven, with tight secrecy laws. They drew in money from many nations. More than 500 banks were registered here and over 17,000 other companies. This picture shows George Town on the island of Grand Cayman.

7 Emancipation – and then?

In 1974 Jessica and Eric Huntley from Guyana co-founded a bookshop in London. It was named after two Caribbean heroes: Bogle-L'Ouverture.

Still poor

Emancipation in the British West Indies in 1838 did not mean that blacks now took over their colony's government (as in Haiti under Toussaint l'Ouverture, see page 16). All the main posts, the big estates, the mansions, the police and the courts remained under white control. As for employment, in that very same year, Sir John Gladstone began to ship low-paid workers from Calcutta to the Caribbean, avoiding any need to pay ex-slaves a good wage.

Newly-freed slaves were now better off in key ways:

- members of the family could not be sold;
- some had scraps of land they could farm;
- if land was available, they now had the right to buy it.

However, most ex-slaves had to start from scratch, owning nothing. There were few hospitals or schools. Yet how could ex-slaves send their children to school in Britain, as planters did? If whites resented the loss of the 'good old days', it was not they who often went hungry or, when there was a drought, faced starvation.

JAMAICA. - For SALE, a valuable SUGAR ESTATE, in the parish of St. James, consisting of upwards of 700 acres, of which 181 acres are canefield, in good condition, and with promising prospects. For further particulars apply to Messrs. Petgrave and Hodgkinson, Solicitors, Bath, and 13, Furnival's-inn, London.

An advertisement in *The Times*, 21 May 1881

Morant Bay, 1865

In the St Thomas parish of Jamaica in 1865, a group of hungry blacks marched to the courthouse in Morant Bay. Led by Paul Bogle, a black Baptist deacon, they wanted to tell the local council about their grievances. However, the chief magistrate would not see them. Instead, he ordered the militia to disperse them. When the demonstrators refused to budge, the militia opened fire, killing several blacks. In the riot that now followed, Bogle and his supporters burned down the courthouse, killed the chief magistrate and several of the militia, then emptied the jail. Edward Eyre, the Governor of Jamaica, responded swiftly and savagely – 439 blacks were killed, hundreds more were flogged. A thousand homes were destroyed. Bogle was hanged from the yardarm of a British ship. W. G. Gordon, a planter of mixed parentage who had ordained Bogle and who sympathised with the rebels, was hanged outside the ruined courthouse. Like many whites in Britain, John Stuart Mill saw Eyre's deeds as murder; others saw them as the only way to keep the British Empire. Charles Dickens, who had criticised slavery in the USA in his novel *Martin Chuzzlewit* (1844), campaigned for Eyre to be given a seat in the House of Lords.

A new day

In his novel *New day* (1949) V. S. Reid uses regional dialect in his fictional version of Jamaica's struggle for self-rule from 1865 up to 1944. The extracts below are from Reid's account of the Morant Bay rebellion, beginning when Paul Bogle and his co-protesters are told to wait quietly until a council banquet is over.

Bogle held up his hands to show that he wants quiet. Quiet comes, then he tells Morant people that he has no' come to the Bay to give them fun, but that he is seeking justice for the poor. 'Hear me now,' he tells them. 'County Inspector says we voices must no' be loud, but sing, we will sing the hymns o' our faith. One o' the brethren will please raise the faithful servants' song: Break Down the Walls o' Jericho.'

But presently I see cook-women carrying platters from the kitchen to the banquet room upstairs. Morant Bay hungry people see it too, and such a howl comes from their hungry bellies!

'You in there a-feast on poor people's money while we out here a-starve!'

The 'white man's burden'

Before freeing slaves in the Caribbean, Britain had developed colonies in other parts of the world – the British Empire grew. The size of the Victorian family grew. Although millions left Britain to settle abroad, the home population still rose between 1811 and 1911 from 13,368,000 to 42,082,000. The proportion of the world's population that was white shot up from an estimated 22 per cent to 35 per cent. British empire-builders such as Cecil Rhodes (1853–1902) felt that this should benefit everybody. In 1881, he said:

❝I contend that we are the first race in the world, and that the more of the world we inhabit, the better it is for the human race. I contend that every acre added to our territory provides for the birth of more of the English race who otherwise would not be brought into existence.❞

Rhodes spoke of 'the English race' and 'the human race'. Others used this un-scientific term 'race' just as loosely. Joseph Chamberlain (called by Churchill 'the architect of Empire' and from 1895 to 1903 Secretary for the Colonies) believed in ' the Anglo-Saxon race'. Sir Francis Younghusband felt morally superior to 'non-Christian races'!

The works of the writer Rudyard Kipling (1865–1936) helped to shape the attitude of generations of whites towards black people, whether in Britain or abroad. An 1899 poem, 'The White Man's Burden', suggests that whites are superior and thus have a duty to help the darker nations. Those born to rule must 'Take up the White Man's burden' and, without expecting thanks, 'Fill full the mouth of Famine/ And bid the sickness cease'.

In 1900, Alfred Milner (later Secretary for the Colonies, 1918–21) said:

❝One of the strongest arguments why the white man must rule is because it is the only possible means of gradually raising the black man, not to our level of civilization, which it is doubtful whether he could ever attain, but up to a much higher level, than that which he at present occupies.❞

The benefits of white rule

In *A History of the English-speaking Peoples* (1958), Sir Winston Churchill quoted Chamberlain's words:

This painting at the National Portrait Gallery in London, c. 1861, is by Thomas Jones Barker. It shows, from left to right, a lady-in-waiting (unidentified), Prince Albert, Queen Victoria, an African chief (unidentified), Viscount Palmerston and Earl Russell.

❝It is not enough to occupy certain great spaces of the world's surface unless you can make the most of them – unless you are willing to develop them. We are landlords of a great estate; it is the duty of a landlord to develop his estate.❞

Churchill commented:

❝Chamberlain could not fulfil this promise in the way he would have wished, though some advances were made, especially in West Africa.❞

Many blacks have been more outspoken in their criticism of British colonial rule. Even leaving aside the atrocities committed on them, they have argued that too much was taken out of the colonies and too little put in. Jomo Kenyatta, for example (who became Kenya's first President when independence was won in 1963), wrote in 1945:

❝There is not one of the boasted blessings of white civilization which has yet been made generally available to the Kenya Africans.❞

Free secondary school education was introduced to Barbados – a colony since 1625 – only in 1961. At the same time 90 per cent of Zambia's children of primary school age were not enrolled in school. While the whites did bring new medicines to their colonies, they also brought new diseases, causing epidemics.

A 1969 census in Jamaica revealed that 300 white landowners, only 0.02 per cent of the population, owned nearly 50 per cent of

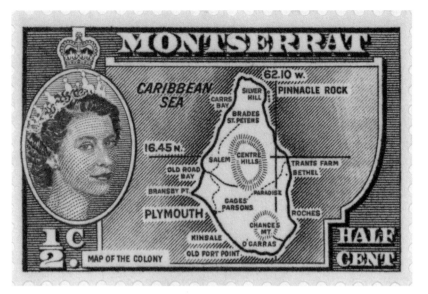

the agricultural land. Could such an imbalance, and the years of underinvestment in the colonies, help to explain why some Afro-Caribbeans came to Britain to seek work or an education?

In Montserrat in 1989, trade union leader Vereen Thomas said, 'We've been a colony for some 300 years now and I don't see the evidence of any benefit from it'.

Under-development

One example: Montserrat

There is little evidence that Britain felt a duty to bring benefits to the black people who had been forced to live in its Caribbean colonies. After the abolition of slavery in 1838, Britain's chief interest in the area remained the same; obtaining raw materials not available more cheaply nearer home. Most investment went into producing items Britain wanted. So long as there were fish in the North Sea, why develop a fishing industry in the Caribbean?

Montserrat, a tiny island of about 100 square kilometres, became a British colony in 1632. African slaves were taken there from 1664 onwards, and by 1772 the population was 1,314 whites and 9,834 black slaves. Throughout all this time, the whites failed to develop the island in a way that would help the majority of its population. The island was geared to grow one main crop for export to Britain: first tobacco, then ginger, sugar, and limes for juice – until each crop fell in price – then cotton. Only one jetty was built: that was all the Mother Country needed. Free schooling

was introduced in Britain in 1870, but not in the colonies: it was not needed for field jobs. Housing for poor people was basic and a hurricane in 1899 left thousands homeless.

Naturally, some blacks left to work abroad; and in the 1950s, when Montserrat's cotton was no longer needed by Britain, and jobs were scarce, going abroad seemed the only answer. Between 1955 and 1961, 3,835 Montserratians came to London, leaving behind a total of only 12,167. (The UK population then was 52,828,085.)

Many settled around Stoke Newington. No matter how low paid they were, most tried to save. They had a duty to their relatives in Montserrat who had no work and no system of unemployment benefit to fall back on. By 1961, the money they were sending to them was four times the sum being earned by the island's cotton trade. If some immigrants in Britain could not afford to 'keep up with the Joneses', it was partly because they were sending aid to a British colony.

Montserrat was not an isolated example. In a report about riots in Jamaica over low wages paid to sugar workers, the *Daily Herald* of 5 May 1938 said:

> 66 A great responsibility rests on the British Administration in Jamaica, which has allowed a deplorably low standard of living to persist in the island. 99

In 1938–9 the British Government sent a team under Lord Moyne, the Secretary for the Colonies, to look at conditions in Jamaica, the Leeward Islands, the Windward Islands, Barbados, Trinidad and Tobago, British Honduras and British Guiana. When the report was published, in 1945, it spoke of poor housing, poor wages, chronic sickness and an education system with 'serious inadequacies in almost every respect'.

Pushed and pulled

The only option for many West Indians was to leave home. If work beckoned, they had always gone. Over 100,000 Jamaicans worked on the construction of the Panama canal. After its completion in 1914, migrants were attracted to the banana plantations of Costa Rica, the sugar estates of Cuba and the oil refineries in the Dutch islands of Curaçao and Aruba. Until shortly after World War II, the USA offered opportunities. In New York, Jamaicans in particular set up many successful businesses. (It was easier there than in Britain, because New York had a much larger black population to trade with.) After a devastating hurricane hit Jamaica in 1951, more people decided to leave. However, in 1952, a new US law cut British West Indian immigration from 65,000 per year to 800. So where else were workers needed? The attractions of the distant Mother Country (even with war-time food-rationing still in force) seemed inviting.

Why did West Indians now seek work in Britain? In short, they were pushed and pulled. What pulled them was the prospect of a job. What pushed them was the situation at home.

Not just nutmeg

As soon as they became independent, some of Britain's former colonies set out to change their countries from a 'one crop' system to something that would benefit more of their people. One economist, Sir Arthur Lewis of St Lucia (1915–91), eventually won a Nobel Prize for his ideas.

Jamaica became independent in 1962. Why should it not make its own aluminium and drinks cans from the massive mineral deposits of bauxite on the island? Grenada became independent in 1974. Interviewed after a political coup in 1979, Bernard Coard, the Deputy Prime Minister, said that only diversification could make Grenada truly independent:

66 First, diversification of agricultural production; secondly, diversification of the markets that we sell these products to; thirdly, diversification of the sources of our tourism, the variety of countries from which our tourists come. Concretely, it means that apart from our cocoa, nutmeg and bananas ... we also want to move into the minor spices area. So that, instead of three, we would have six or seven basic food items to export. We need to develop a fishing industry. We also want to process these foodstuffs ourselves. 99

The black-led government of Grenada found it hard to diversify as it wished. In particular, the US government was unwilling to see the country develop links with Cuba and the Soviet Union. Acute political struggles within Grenada added to the island's problems until, in October 1983, US troops invaded.

In Britain, many people compared the British government's acceptance of this inva-

Slums in Kingston, Jamaica.

sion with their actions in 1982, when some other islands with ties to the British crown – but with white citizens – were invaded. A white journalist, Peregrine Worsthorne, in the *Sunday Telegraph* of 23 May 1982, commented:

66 If the Falkland Islanders were British citizens with black or brown skins, spoke with strange accents or worshipped different Gods, it is doubtful whether the Royal Navy and Marines would today be fighting for their liberation. 99

On 27 June 1982 Worsthorne wrote:

66 Most Britons today identify more easily with those of the same stock 8,000 miles away ... than they do with West Indian or Asian immigrants living next door. 99

If Worsthorne was right, did this help to explain the policy of neglect so long practised by Britain in the Caribbean?

8 Solidarity

From continent to continent

In the USA, slavery north of the Ohio River ended by 1787; but 4 million slaves were still held in the Southern states. It would take a civil war (1861–1865) to free them. Until then, Britain was a haven for some slaves, including Ellen Croft, a brave and clever woman who had been a slave in Georgia. Her skin was so light in colour that nobody could tell she was a slave. Her husband, William, was much darker. In 1848, when they were to be parted and forced to work for different planters, Ellen hatched a daring plan. Dressing up as a man, she pretended to be a slaveholder. Then, with William acting as her servant, they bluffed their way north to Philadelphia and eventually sought refuge in Britain.

During this period Britain was also visited by free African-Americans who were campaigning to end slavery at home, and wanted support from friends abroad. Britain was, after all, responsible for allowing slaves into its American colonies in the first place, and had taken countless captives there via the Caribbean. The most impressive of the campaigners was Frederick Douglass. He toured Britain several times between 1847 and 1860, speaking to packed meetings everywhere.

Had Douglass gone to the theatre, he might have seen a fellow-countryman in a starring role. Ira Aldridge (1807–1867) was a free-born New Yorker, the son of a lay preacher and grandson of a slave. After working his way to Liverpool as a steward, he had settled in London in 1825. He married a Yorkshire woman and, despite racist abuse from some theatre critics, went on to become a famous actor. He did not limit himself to black roles – like Othello or Aaron in *Titus Andronicus* –but also played Lear and Macbeth. He won acclaim in the provinces and in many of Europe's capitals. After starring as Shylock during a tour of Russia, speaking lines he surely felt – such as 'If you prick us, do we not bleed? If you tickle us, do we not laugh?' – he was thanked by a party of Jews for portraying the character as a human being.

Support of a different kind was given by Aldridge's second daughter, Amanda. She was still living in London in 1925, when the African-American actor and singer Paul Robeson, son of a former slave, arrived in Britain. She gave him the ear-rings her father had worn as Othello, urging Robeson to play the role and wear them.

A statue of US President Abraham Lincoln in Manchester carries a text, dated 19 January 1863, praising the 'Christian heroism' of the working people of the city, the mill workers, who supported Lincoln by boycotting cotton from slaveholding states of the South.

Right: An American advertisement for a runaway slave.

$150 REWARD

RANAWAY from the subscriber, on the night of the 2d instant, a negro man, who calls himself *Henry May*, about 22 years old, 5 feet 6 or 8 inches high, ordinary color, rather chunky built, bushy head, and has it divided mostly on one side, and keeps it very nicely combed; has been raised in the house, and is a first rate dining-room servant, and was in a tavern in Louisville for 18 months. I expect he is now in Louisville trying to make his escape to a free state, (in all probability to Cincinnati, Ohio.) Perhaps he may try to get employment on a steamboat. He is a good cook, and is handy in any capacity as a house servant. Had on when he left, a dark cassinett coatee, and dark striped cassinett pantaloons, new---he had other clothing. I will give $50 reward if taken in Louisvill; 100 dollars if taken one hundred miles from Louisville in this State, and 150 dollars if taken out of this State, and delivered to me, or secured in any jail so that I can get him again. WILLIAM BURKE.

Bardstown, Ky., September 3d, 1838.

A tailor from Kent

It was not only for the rights of blacks that Britain's Afro-Caribbeans worked. William Cuffay (1788–1870) was born in Chatham, a naval base near London, in the year that Britain began transporting convicts to New South Wales. His father was an ex-slave from St Kitts who worked as a cook on a warship. William, however, became a tailor. He was always active and keen to help others. He joined a trade union, and was sacked for going on strike. He saw a need for MPs who were more in sympathy with ordinary working people. In 1839 he became a supporter of the Chartist movement. He demanded six reforms: voting by secret ballot; electoral districts of equal size; all adult males to have the vote; wages for MPs; an end to the rule that only men with property could become MPs; and annual parliaments. He organised protest marches and was a rousing speaker. Then, in 1848, the little tailor was charged with planning a violent revolt. Despite his denials, he was sentenced to be transported for life to Tasmania. In court, he said:

> 66 I know that a great many men of good moral character are now suffering in prison only for advocating the cause of the Charter; but, however, I do not despair of its being carried out. I know my cause is good, and therefore I think I can endure any punishment proudly. I feel no disgrace at being called a felon. 99

Another black who was involved in the unrest of the time was Joseph Thomas. The *Manchester Guardian* of 24 August 1842 reports how a group of men including Thomas, 'a man of colour', appeared in court accused of taking part in a riot and throwing stones at the windows of a mill. While Thomas denied that he had thrown 'upwards of twenty' stones, he was the only one of the accused who admitted that he had thrown any at all?

Service in the Crimea

Jamaican-born Mary Seacole (1805–1881) sold goods and provided medical aid to troops in the thick of the Crimean War (1854–1856). Many people in Britain know only of a white nurse, Florence Nightingale, who worked in that war, the 'lady with the lamp'. Soldiers in the field knew Mrs Seacole, however, and they showed how grateful they were. When she settled in London after the War with little money, she was helped by a benefit concert organised by Crimean veterans – senior officers as well as other ranks – eleven military bands turned out to play for her. Her obituary in *The Times*, 21 May 1888, said:

> 66 She was present at many battles, and at the risk of her life often carried the wounded off the field. 99

Solidarity was on display in 1987, when newly-elected MP Diane Abbott (left) and US civil rights campaigner Angela Davis (right) shared a platform with Bience Gawanas of the South West African People's Organisation. Two years later, as Namibia moved to independence, police from Jamaica were proud to join the UN forces monitoring the transition.

A bust of Mary Seacole made by a nephew of Queen Victoria.

An extract from *The Times*, 2 October 1848.

Binding her diverse peoples

Many prominent historical figures have had a foreign-born parent or partner, including Bonnie Prince Charlie, Queen Victoria, Sir Winston Churchill and Elizabeth II. Henry VIII, of course, had more than one. Rudyard Kipling, though born overseas, was not an 'alien'. Britain had no restrictive laws on nationality or immigration during the long reign of Victoria (1837–1901). As the British Empire expanded, all the peoples within its vast borders were viewed as 'British subjects', whatever their country of origin.

This did not mean there was just one way of life. Whites in the colonies and blacks settling in Britain felt no need to adopt all the local customs of their new home. Equally, when Queen Victoria encouraged immigration to Britain by employing Indians to serve her, she saw no reason for them to dress other than in their traditional fashion. The Queen, Churchill wrote:

> 66 sent her sons and grandsons on official tours of her ever-increasing dominions, where they were heartily welcomed. Homage from a stream of colonial dignitaries was received by her in England. She appointed Indian servants to her household, and from them learnt Hindustani. Thus she sought by every means within her power to bind her diverse peoples together in loyalty to the British Crown. 99

The example set by the Royal Family, some feel, is still important. In *The Changing Anatomy of Britain* (1982), Anthony Sampson notes how:

> 66 (Prince Charles) has a black girl secretary on his private staff, but many people concerned with race relations think that the Palace should go further by appointing a black aide or equerry who could more visibly demonstrate that monarchy has no racial bias. 99

From *The Times* of 21 May 1888.

The trustees of the fund established some time since in behalf of Mrs. Mary Seacole wish it to be known that she died on the 14th inst. The deceased, it will be remembered, greatly distinguished herself as a nurse on the battlefield and in hospitals during the Crimean war. A Creole, she was born in Jamaica early in the present century, and from childhood was instructed by her mother in the art of nursing. In 1855, after it had been announced that no more nurses were required in the Crimea, she established a mess-table and comfortable quarters for sick and convalescent officers at Balaclava, landing there in the month of February. She was present at many battles, and at the risk of her life often carried the wounded off the field.

Abdul Karim (1863–1909) served Queen Victoria, the Empress of India, from 1887 until her death in 1901.

A change in meaning

From the 1950s to the 1970s, about two-thirds of the immigrants to Britain were black, one-third white. Whatever the exact proportions, the term immigrant somehow came to mean 'black' – with the term used equally to include balcks born here. Oddly, some whites took to hurling the word about as an insult. (It is worth pointing out that from 1952, the heir to the British throne was the son of an immigrant – and he was not the first. Together with his two black servants, Mehemet and Mustafa a white immigrant arrived in London in the eighteenth century. His parents were not British, nor was his wife, and he never learned to speak English. All the same, as George I he was King of Great Britain and Ireland from 1714 to 1727; his son was King from 1727 to 1760; and his great-grandson reigned from 1760 to 1820

A Victorian custom

In his *History of the English-Speaking Peoples* (1957) Sir Winston Churchill wrote:

> 66 The dawn of the twentieth century seemed bright for those who lived within the unequalled bounds of the British Empire, or sought shelter within its folds. 99

Among those seeking shelter in Britain were sailors from the Caribbean, who were hired when any ship from Britain needed to take on crew. New technology in the form of steamships and the telegraph changed the nature of seafaring; but British ship-owners continued to want a supply of low-waged seamen, particularly below decks as stokers or 'firemen'. When their ship left Britain again, those still under contract left with them. Others were paid off and left behind. Some blacks remained behind voluntarily, preferring to look for better pay on a new ship or to settle in Britain – or to do both, since seamen based in Britain were paid more than those hired abroad. If they stayed, they usually lived in the black communities near the docks, not only in London, Liverpool and Bristol, but in Cardiff's Butetown or 'Tiger Bay', in Newport, South Shields or Glasgow. They were conforming to a custom typical of the Victorian era: as British subjects, just like whites, they were exercising their right to settle wherever they liked within the Empire.

J. R. Archer, a seaman's son

Britain's very first non-white MPs were British subjects from India, living in London, who spent much time demanding home rule for India and lobbying on behalf of workers in the British West Indies and in South Africa. They were: Dadabhai Naoroji (who was an MP from 1892 to 1895), Sir Mancherjee Bhownagree (1895–1906) and Shapurji Saklatvala (1922–23, 1924–29). Helping Saklatvala to become an MP in 1922, as his agent, was J. R. Archer, who also had strong views on Britain's colonies.

John Richard Archer (1863–1932) was born in Liverpool. He was the son of a white Irishwoman and a black seaman from Barbados. Archer was a photographer, and he set up a studio in London, where he was active in politics. He was the first Englishman of Afro-Caribbean descent to be elected as a borough councillor in 1906. He went on to become Mayor of Battersea – Britain's first black mayor – in 1913.

In 1918 he was elected as the first President of the African Progress Union (APU). Its aims were to promote the welfare of 'Afro-Peoples', to spread knowledge of their history and their achievements, and to foster 'brotherhood in its broadest sense'. In his first speech to the APU in 1918, he demanded that blacks in the colonies be allowed to govern themselves, arguing that, if white rule had been so beneficial, surely blacks were ready for any role by now?

A gifted Londoner

Samuel Coleridge-Taylor (1875–1912) was born in Holborn, London. His mother was white and his father was a doctor from Sierra Leone. Coleridge-Taylor was a child prodigy. He could read music by the age of four, and was sent to the Royal College of Music at 15. By the age of 24 he was conducting his own work at the Royal Albert Hall, highly praised by Elgar.

Coleridge-Taylor enjoyed enormous personal success, but he was not content to think only of himself. He wanted justice for all black people, here and abroad. From 1900 he was active in the Pan African Association (whose inspiration was the African-American academic W. E. B. DuBois). Coleridge-Taylor set to music some poems by Paul Laurence Dunbar, the son of a former slave. He gave concerts in the USA, and was invited to the

The crew of the *Cawdor* in San Francisco in 1893 after a five-month voyage from Liverpool, black and white on deck together now. In the decade up to 1793, by contrast, 878 ships from Liverpool carried 303,738 slaves to the New World.

Good Company
present

**CROWNED
WITH FAME**

BY
MICHAEL ELLIS and GOOD COMPANY
A rediscovery of SAMUEL COLERIDGE TAYLOR

ON TOUR September - November, 1987

WORLD PREMIERE

Good Company
present

**CROWNED
WITH FAME**

Written by
MICHAEL ELLIS
A rediscovery of the life and music of

Directed by
SUE POMEROY

Coleridge-Taylor's life was cut short by pneumonia, and his music fell out of fashion. However, a modern play about him, *Crowned with Fame* (1987), rekindled interest in audiences throughout Britain.

White House by President Theodore Roosevelt. Writing on him in 1904, Booker T. Washington said:

> 66 Using some of the native songs of Africa and the West Indies with songs that came into being in America during the slavery regime, he has in handling these melodies preserved their distinctive traits and individuality, at the same time giving them an art form fully imbued with their essential spirit. 99

Doctors at work

Black people have made many notable contributions in the field of medicine. The first successful operation on the human heart, for example, was performed by an African-American, Dr Daniel Hale Williams, in Chicago in 1893. Another African-American doctor, Charles Drew, was later known as 'the father of the blood bank'. Nonetheless, blacks have often struggled to be accepted as doctors, not least in Britain.

A few blacks, such as Dr Theophilus Scholes, were able to train here in the nineteenth century and then work abroad; but finding work here was hard. Samuel Coleridge-Taylor's father, for example, returned to Sierra Leone. There were, of course, several black communities in which black doctors could set up a practice. The problem here (before the National Health Service was set up in 1948) was that few blacks could afford to pay expensive doctor's fees. Yet, if black doctors earned too little, how could they afford modern equipment or keep in touch with medical research – which was difficult enough anyway if they were snubbed by their white colleagues? If they failed to keep up to date, it might eventually be true that black doctors were only second-best.

To stay in business, black doctors had to be wealthy themselves or to be accepted by at least some patients who could pay well, which meant whites. Unfortunately, to most whites, blacks were unfamiliar and did not inspire confidence. Outside certain areas, most whites seldom saw a black person. Even in the 1980s, when one Briton in a hundred was an Afro-Caribbean, the percentage of any local population that was black was about nil in most small towns and villages, or over 50 per cent, in just a handful of inner cities. Half of Britain's Afro-Caribbeans were concentrated in the poorest boroughs of London.

46

It was not until the early twentieth century that Afro-Caribbean doctors made their mark in Britain – through a combination of skill, character, good fortune and hard work. As well as tackling disease and illness, and coping with personal discrimination, they strove to improve conditions for other blacks in Britain and campaigned for self-government in the colonies. Some spoke out loudly, others worked in quieter ways.

John Alcindor (1873–1924)

Present at Coleridge-Taylor's funeral, and at a wedding of the composer's daughter in 1922, was Dr John Alcindor. He was a Catholic from Trinidad, who had won a scholarship to study in Edinburgh in 1893 and had qualified as a doctor in 1899. He had settled in Paddington, where he was one of the four district medical officers, and had married a nurse, a white Londoner. In addition to his daily work, he found time to write medical papers on influenza, cancer and tuberculosis, play cricket (as a wicket-keeper) and still devote a lot of energy to politics. From 1900 he was active in the Pan-African Association; and in 1921 he took over from John Archer as leader of the African Progress Union. During World War I his services were not wanted by the British army because he was 'of colonial origin', so he worked with the Red Cross, an organisation officially represented at his funeral.

Harold Moody (1882–1947)

Harold Moody left Jamaica in 1904 to study at King's College Hospital in London. Then as now, the Caribbean could not offer the same facilities as Europe. The prizes he won as a student made it no easier for him to rent a room or, after qualifying in 1910, to get a job. He was turned down at King's when the matron refused to have a black doctor on the staff; and he was deemed unsuitable for a job in a poor area of Camberwell, because white patients would be unhappy with 'a nigger to attend them'. In 1913, Dr Moody set up his own practice in Peckham. He earned less then a pound in his first week, but he persevered and became established.

Through the League of Coloured Peoples, which he formed in 1931, he pressed for self-government in the colonies; but he also attended to the welfare of black people in Britain. Every summer he took coachloads of poor black children to the seaside and at Christmas he organised a party for them.

During World War II he worked in civil defence in London, but continued to demand fair conditions for the blacks who came to support the war effort. Like John Alcindor's son Cyril, Dr Moody's children had 'war-time commissions' in the forces: his daughter was a doctor and two of his sons were promoted to the rank of major. No doubt Dr Moody was proud of them; but it was not good enough, he told the Government, that blacks could be made officers in an emergency yet not in peacetime.

A doctor in Hackney

James Jackson Brown (1882–1953) was born in Jamaica and claimed Maroon ancestry. After studying in Canada, he completed his training in London, assisting a number of well-known white doctors, one of whom later became the personal physician to George V. In 1914 he set up his own practice. While a student he had lodged in Hackney with a Jewish family and it was his landlord's daughter, Milly Green, whom he married. Their home attracted people from the black community and whites, too, with bridge, music and conversation on offer. 'JJ' also formed an all-black cricket team, the Africs, which played twice a week all around London in the 1920s and 1930s. During World War II he worked with the St John's Ambulance Brigade and helped bomb victims; his son Leslie worked in the aircraft industry.

Dr Brown forged links between blacks and Jews in Hackney before World War I. Such links also exist today. In 1989, as this photo shows, the Mayor of Hackney, Medlin Lewis, entertained a group from Israel on an exchange visit.

9 Two wars

World War I

Blacks resident in Britain as well as blacks from the West Indies, the Bermudas and Africa served with the British forces on land and at sea during the First World War. They fought under white officers in regiments such as the British West Indies Regiment, the Gold Coast Regiment and the King's African Rifles. Over 1,000 black seamen based in Cardiff alone lost their lives. Many more were killed or wounded, and many were awarded medals.

A poster, 1919.

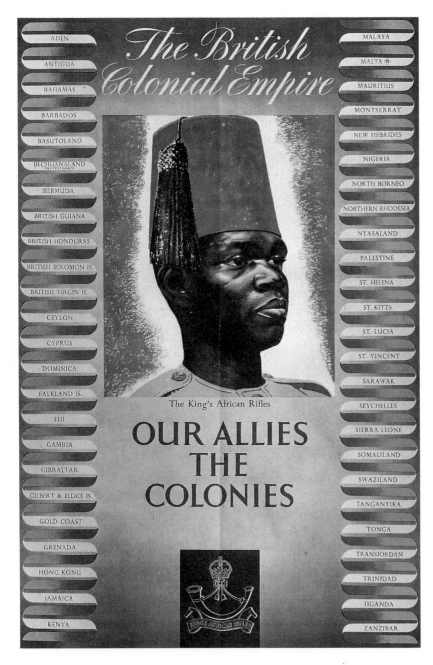

Gallant comrades

The Times of 13 June 1919 acknowledged that: '(black seamen) had faced the perils of the submarine campaign with all the gallantry of British seamen'. This was praise, yet the words were similar to those in Kipling's poem about Gunga Din (see page 22); and did they imply that blacks were not British?

Hopes of equal treatment after the war were in vain. Black troops were even kept out of the victory celebrations, including the Peace March through London on 19 July 1919.

Not ready?

Speaking as President of the African Progress Union in 1918, and recalling the sacrifices made by black people in the First World War, John Archer said:

66 (We have been told that this war has been) for the self-determination of small nations and the freedom of the world from the despotism of German rule. The truth of that statement will be proved by the way they deal in America with Afro-Americans, in France with their Negro subjects, in Belgium with their Congo subjects, and in Great Britain with India, Africa and the West Indies. We shall be told the old, old story. Africa is not ready; the time is not ripe; they are not sufficiently advanced ... 99

When many of Europe's black colonies did eventually become independent, after World War II, their problems were not over. Economically and militarily they were weak; and in some parts of Africa and Asia atrocities were committed on a large scale. In May 1989 the cry 'Death to the Moors!' came not from whites but during violence between Senegalese and

"What right have the whites anywhere to teach us about democracy, when they executed those who asked for democracy during the time of colonial rule?"

Nelson Mandela

Mauritanians. In the Caribbean, too, murder occurred all too often – as in the Jamaican election campaign of 1980, when 700 people died. Nonetheless, if any whites thought such incidents proved blacks were less ready to rule than white-led nations, they only needed to recall the massacre by the British in Amritsrar in India in 1919, the purges carried out under Stalin, the holocaust under Hitler or the deeds of US troops at My Lai in Vietnam in March 1968.

A stamp marking the return of West Indian troops, 1919.

These headlines are from *The Times*, 7 June 1919.

LIVERPOOL COLOURED MEN TO BE INTERNED.

POLICE COURT CHARGES.

COLOURED MISSIONARY'S PLEA.

BLACK AND WHITE AT LIVERPOOL SUNDAY NIGHT OUTBREAK

AT NEWPORT AND LIVERPOOL.

CARDIFF RACE RIOTS.

IRISHMAN AND NEGRO SHOT.

NEGROES BEATEN WITH FRYING-PANS.

CHARLES WOOTTON CENTRE   FOR FURTHER EDUCATION 051·708·9698

In 1978 Charles Wootton's name was chosen for an education centre not far from the docks where he died.

After World War I

Thousands of troops from the colonies were demobilized (demobbed) at ports in Britain, where they had to wait for transport to their home country. In many cases they had no money, since they had to wait for back pay to be issued to them. Few were treated as heroes while they waited. Blacks who lived in Britain found, too, on returning to civilian life, that they still faced discrimination. Over a thousand were unemployed in Cardiff and even more in Liverpool, where shipping companies gave first preference to white seamen. Some blacks were even denied the 'out-of-work donation' to which they were entitled. Had their contribution to the war effort not earned them better treatment than this? Many whites did not think so. On the contrary, in 1919, in London and in other ports, white mobs proved eager to remind blacks of 'their place'.

In Liverpool there was a week-long riot, following a fight between a group of blacks and some white seamen. White mobs, thousands strong, attacked every black they saw, looting and setting fire to their lodgings. There were many stabbings. One young West Indian, recently-demobbed, a ship's fireman called Charles Wootton, was chased to the docks and drowned.

From the trenches to Wales

When mobs attacked the black community in Newport, South Wales, in 1919, the rioting was apparently because a black man had been seen with a white woman. A similar attack on blacks in Cardiff's Butetown may also have been sparked off by whites angry at seeing some black men out with some white women. In a week of violence, homes were set on fire and men killed. Even ex-servicemen from the British West Indies Regiment, still in uniform, were attacked. It made no difference that the women seen at the outset of the riot were actually married to the black men they were with!

Among the recently demobbed black men in South Wales in 1919 was a 31-year-old doctor, working in Pontypridd. Rufus Fennell from Trinidad had served in the trenches and despite being wounded three times had treated countless British troops in Mesopotamia. Now he became a spokesman for the besieged blacks of South Wales, calling upon them to stay within the law but to defend themselves. When he accused the Cardiff police of doing too little to protect blacks, and the Government of sending some ex-servicemen home to the colonies without giving them the pay they were owed, he found himself in court on a trumped-up charge. But he was freed.

When first-hand accounts of the race riots in Britain were taken back to the West Indies by returning ex-servicemen, riots broke out and there were calls for self-government and the expulsion of all whites. In Wales, white seamen, were unmoved. The Trades Union Congress of 1930 passed the following resolution put forward by delegates from Cardiff:

66 That this Congress views with alarm the continued employment of alien and undesirable coloured labour on British ships to the detriment of British seamen and calls upon the Government to use all their powers to provide remedial action. 99

Not cricket?

Learie Constantine

Viv Richards

Learie Constantine (1901–71) was born in Trinidad. His grandfather had been a slave. In 1929 Constantine came to the little town of Nelson in Lancashire and played cricket for the local club for nine seasons. In the words of an adoring cricket fan, a white man, who even in 1987 still remembered those days:

66 He brought 'magic' to the town at a time when the local cotton industry was depressed. At nearby clubs, fewer than 100 spectators paid to watch. At Nelson, when Learie Constantine played, the crowd could be up to 12,000. 99

C. L. R. James, who lived with the Constantines in Nelson for a while, has pointed out that the game of cricket gave young men from the under-developed Caribbean islands a chance to make their way in the world. Certainly Constantine was successful. He worked for the Ministry of Labour during World War II, qualified as a barrister, and became Minister of Transport in Trinidad & Tobago. He was knighted in 1962, then in 1969 he was made a lord: Baron Constantine of Maraval and Nelson.

Despite the lasting joy he brought to cricket fans, Constantine remained a target for racist abuse. His response was to fight. When London's Imperial Hotel did not want to give him a room, in 1943, and he was called a 'nigger', he took the hotel to court. After a lengthy battle he won. As *The Times* of 29 June 1944 reported, the court found

66 that Mr Constantine was ... a British subject from the West Indies, and that, although he was a man of colour, no ground existed on which the defendants were entitled to refuse to receive and lodge him. 99

Learie Constantine had won this case, but winning hearts was harder, as he made clear in a book, *The Colour Bar* (1954):

66 Most British people would be quite unwilling for a black man to enter their homes, nor would they wish to work with one as a colleague, nor to stand shoulder to shoulder with one at a factory bench. 99

Other West Indian cricket stars to play in the Lancashire League include George Headley, Everton Weekes, Clive Lloyd, Wes Hall, Charlie Griffiths and Michael Holding. In 1987 Viv Richards of Antigua, the captain of the West Indies, followed, bringing 'magic' and enormous crowds to a small town in Lancashire called Rishton. In 1988, he revealed that he was following in the footsteps of Learie Constantine in another sense, too:

'A lot of things go through a man's mind when they make him captain of the West Indies. He thinks of all those people who maybe don't have a great life. So many West Indians in England, bus drivers, guys who work on the Underground, you know what I mean? Maybe their cricket team can give them a little bit of pride. When they're talking with English fellers, they can say: "Yeah, but did you see what we did to you at Lord's or the Oval?" Very important to them, that is.'

Fighting fascism

Blacks from all over the world served with the British forces in World War II, including thousands from the Caribbean and a million and a half Indians. Afro-Caribbeans played many different roles. As civilians in Britain they did duty at air-raid shelters and worked in munitions factories and hospitals. Some were army cooks, clerks or aircraft technicians. Billy Strachan from Jamaica served in the RAF as a pilot and flew on more than 40 missions over Europe. Eight hundred lumberjacks from Belize (then British Honduras) came to Scotland's forests to produce timber for the war effort. For some, Italy's invasion of Ethiopa was a special reason to fight the fascists.

In the factories, some blacks soon gained respect from their white workmates. After their shift, however, they found few pubs or clubs would welcome them. An exception was the Ethiopian Teashop in Manchester. This was run by Guianan-born Ras Makonnen (who had changed his name from George Griffith).

Socially, the situation was made worse by the million or so white troops from the USA based in Britain from 1942. They brought with them their custom of segregation, which many British pubs and clubs adopted in order to do business. 130,000 black GIs came over, too, serving in separate black regiments, and some people in Britain welcomed them, some even married them, but it was the whites who set the tone. They had the most money to spend. If white Americans favoured a dance-hall or pub, then black men found themselves barred from it, even if they were British subjects wearing His Majesty's uniform. The hotel that barred Learie Constantine in 1943 was full of white US officers.

Attached to one US black artillery division as a war correspondent was the musician Rudolph Dunbar (1907–88) whose grandparents had been slaves in British Guiana. Dunbar not only covered the Normandy invasion – but gave a concert after the liberation of Paris in 1944 and conducted the Berlin Philharmonic Orchestra in September 1945 after the liberation of Berlin.

After World War II

On the eve of Remembrance Sunday 1987, journalist Leslie Goffe spoke to members of the West Indian Ex-Serviceman's Association in Britain and the interviews appeared in *The Guardian* on 7 November:

One of the panels at Brookwood Cemetery, near Woking

66 I. E. Fairweather is perhaps the most decorated soldier among them. He is was with the 8th Army in Egypt, Tanganyika and Italy. There, he remembers, his unit dug trenches and buried the dead. 'The hospitality was magnificent from the English in 1943,' he says emphatically. But by the time he returned to Britain after being demobbed in Jamaica things had changed. 'They hated the very sight of you, once it was over,' he says. 'But I say if I am good enough to die in your wars, then I am good enough to live with you.' The director of the Association, Neil Flanagan recalls how the race issue was used to encourage their participation. 'We were told that Hitler was a tyrant and that black people would suffer most if he captured the world.' 99

In *Down at the Cross* (1962), James Baldwin wrote: 'White people were, and are, astounded by the holocaust in Germany. They did not know that they could act that way. But I doubt very much whether black people were astounded – at least, in the same way.'

10 A mixed welcome

Recruited again

Immediately after the Second World War, Britain had to rebuild its economy, just as its trading rivals were doing, and it had to repay huge debts to the USA.

It was no use relying on profits from the Empire. Instead, the Government decided to create wealth at home and, where there were gaps in the workforce, to bring in extra workers. Some were Yemenis from Aden, others came from Somalia or the British West Indies.

The first Afro-Caribbeans to answer this call were actually already in Britain; ex-servicemen waiting for transport home after being demobbed. Aware of the conditions that awaited them in the neglected colonies, they decided to settle in the Mother Country – which, until the law was changed in 1962, any Commonwealth citizen had the right to do. To re-build Britain quickly, however, far more workers were needed. In London, where the cost of living was high, they were needed as porters, cleaners, drivers, and nurses – jobs that paid so badly that few whites wanted them. In the Midlands, semi-skilled workers were needed in the furnaces and forges of the manufacturing industries which were all set to expand. Jamaican-born Bill Morris, Deputy General Secretary of Britain's largest trade union, the Transport and General Workers' Union, wrote in 1988: 'Such jobs, not surprisingly, were dirty and dangerous and those with a high rate of anti-social shift work'. The first job in post-war Britain for Flight-Lieutenant Billy Strachan (see page 51) was sweeping the floor in a factory.

Needed, yes – but wanted?

In June 1948, the SS *Empire Windrush* docked in Britain. Coming ashore were 492 job-seekers from Jamaica, mostly ex-servicemen. Given a warm welcome by the press and in cinema newsreels, they soon found work via the labour exchange in Brixton, which is where they settled; and more boats followed. To their amazement, the new arrivants found the general public less keen to welcome them than the cameras had been. In Liverpool, where thousands of sailors were out of work, violence broke out in August 1948. White mobs attacked the hostels where West Indians were staying.

As the ecomomy grew, more workers were needed nonetheless. Peter Fryer, who saw the SS *Empire Windrush* dock, noted (in *Staying Power*, 1984):

66 In April 1956 London Transport began recruiting staff in Barbados, and within 12 years a total of 3,787 Barbadians had been taken on. They were lent their fares to Britain, and the loans were repaid gradually from their wages. Even this number was not enough, and in 1966 London Transport would begin to recruit in Trinidad and Jamaica too. The British Hotels and Restaurants Association recruited skilled workers in Barbados. And a Tory Health Minister by the name of Enoch Powell welcomed West Indian nurses to Britain. Willing black hands drove tube trains, collected bus fares, emptied hospital patients' bed-pans. 99

Workers arriving on the SS *Empire Windrush*, Tilbury, 22 June 1948.

A changing society

Other countries in western Europe had a labour shortage. Together with Britain, in the first two decades after the war, they sucked in some 11 million workers from abroad (about 5 per cent of the total workforce). What was happening in Britain was not unique; and it was not only in Britain that there were whites not ready to welcome black newcomers.

Some whites in Britain, especially men, could hardly adjust to the post-war world at all. It was changing so fast. Women had proved during the war that they could do many jobs once done by men. Now, between 1951 and 1971, over two million women joined the workforce (dwarfing the number of new immigrants). Another social revolution was the slum clearance that split up old-established communities. After 1956 Britain's days as a superpower were over. The USA and its youth cultures exerted ever more influence. Wider car ownership altered people's customs and their lives.

It was into this situation that Britain's newest wave of immigrants came. If they want to live here, they should fit in, many whites said. But what were they fitting in to? The old ways were constantly challenged.

Some blacks fresh from the Caribbean colonies were amazed to see white men as porters, carrying passengers' suitcases at ports and railway stations, and white women scrubbing floors or doorsteps. The new arrivants nonetheless expected to fit in here quite easily. They spoke English; they shared a love of national sports like football and cricket; and most were Christians who took their Bible seriously. In *A savage culture* (1981) a 1953 arrivant, Remi Kapo, quotes a tip West Indians received from the BBC: 'People will grow to respect you more if they see you often in the church.' But how many whites went to church any more and would see you?

Many blacks were bewildered, not only by the cold welcome they received, but by the apparent lack of Christian values that prevailed. Britain's motto in 1959 was 'You've never had it so good' and the 'Swinging Sixties' brought in new morals. One Afro-Caribbean response, as soon as families were settled, was to establish black-led churches, where their traditions could be maintained.

Io Smith came from Jamaica in the 1950s as a 20-year-old. Thirty years on, now a pastor of the New Testament Church in London, she recalled: 'I brought my faith with me – and a good job I did, because I hardly could find it here'.

Minette Bailey said:

> It is very strange to see how many people flock inside the pubs on Sunday instead of going to worship God. It is very strange how many English missionaries came to the West Indies to teach us about God, yet when we came here we found out that the white people do not love God, as many black Londoners.

In 1982, the Archbishop of Canterbury, Robert Runcie, acknowledged this:

> The presence of the ethnic groups with their different religious traditions has given new breadth and generosity to our vision of the brotherhood of man and the fatherhood of God. The new arrivals from Asia, Africa and the Caribbean have sometimes been blamed for the incoherence of Britain, but in reality British society was in the process of being atomised long before they arrived. What coherence there was has decayed under the impact of materialism and assertive self-interest. The immigrants bring rich gifts.

Jamaican-born Pastor F. S. Wallen and Mrs Wallen of the Church of God, Brixton, 1961.

One of the Caribbean immigrants who swept Britain's streets in the '60s.

53

Grin and bear it?

When the new recruits arrived from the Caribbean, with its bright skies and warm colours, they had to come to terms with the greyness of Britain's streets and the coldness of the people. Mostly young men at first, they had arrived full of hope – to be greeted by boarding-house signs saying: 'NO COLOUREDS' or 'NO BLACKS, NO DOGS, NO IRISH'. In novels, plays and poems, black writers have painted a bleak picture of this period. They faced the twin pressure of separation from their families and the cold shoulder at work or in the pub. Because of this intense double pressure, some medical studies have suggested, Afro-Caribbeans ran a risk of becoming ill. Most survived by telling themselves that it was only for a few years; once they had saved some money, they would return to a warmer climate. Others resolved to stay, save up and re-unite their family in Britain. Many had to rely on black solidarity or a sense of humour.

A character in *Sweet and Sour Milk* (1979), a novel by Nuruddin Farah of Somalia, says: 'Raise your children, but not your voice nor your head. To survive, you must clown'. Certainly, Bill Lewis from St Vincent found his sense of humour an asset when he was a bus conductor in Oxford in the 1960s. Years later, in 1990, he recalled one incident when his word had not been trusted:

❝The rather posh woman passenger decided to take a second opinion, after asking me whether my bus was going to the station. So she went round to the front of the bus, to ask the same question of the driver, an Irishman. When she came back, her query now confirmed by both of us, I grinned broadly and said: 'Well now, ma'am, are you happy now that you've got it in black and white?' All the passengers on the bus roared with laughter. That's how barriers get broken down.❞

Fear of competition?

Whites expressing hostility to blacks often accused them of disliking work and just wanting to scrounge on the dole or – at the same time – of being so keen to work, even for low pay, that they took jobs away from whites! In the 1940s and 1950s outright hostility came first from unskilled white men – less able to move into the fresh openings or less mobile – and from trade unionists hoping to use the labour shortage as a lever to obtain better pay. A motion put to the Trades Union Congress in 1958 said:

❝It is time a stop was put to all foreign labour entering this country. In the event of a slump occurring, the market would be flooded with cheap foreign labour ... a serious deterrent to trade union bargaining power.❞

Whites who were more highly qualified – stockbrokers, diplomats, judges – were less openly hostile to the influx of black workers; but then they had no rooms to let and did not work on the shop floor or on the buses. It may be that they never even travelled by bus. Their welcome would be tested later, when blacks began to aim higher. (In the field of law, for example, a survey of career opportunities for black lawyers, published in 1989 by a High Court judge, Mr Justice Steyn, found that 'racial disadvantage exists at the Bar'.)

Bill Lewis, a bus conductor for many years, became Oxford's first-ever black bus inspector.

Finding a place

In 1990 Clive Walker, now a taxi-driver, recalled his arrival in Birmingham from the West Indies in the early 1960s. By then the signs in boarding-house windows had changed. Instead of 'NO BLACKS' they said: ROOM TO LET.

> Of course when I knocked and asked about the room, I was told it had just gone. But for days afterwards I'd walk past that same house and see the advert still up in the window: ROOM TO LET.

Turned away from private lodgings by an unofficial colour bar, and obliged to wait five years for low-cost council housing, many low-paid Afro-Caribbeans had no choice but to rent rooms in a slum. Even then, many could only afford to share one room with fellow blacks, no matter how overcrowded and stressful. If they tried to buy or rent homes in better areas, by pooling their resources with partners, some families were abused or attacked. Not trusting the police to protect them, most stayed in 'black areas' of London or other big cities, including Toxteth (Liverpool 8), St Paul's (Bristol), Butetown (Cardiff), Chapeltown (Leeds), Handsworth (Birmingham) and Moss Side (Manchester). Their parents may have worked in rural areas in the Caribbean, but few of Britain's Afro-Caribbeans lived in the country now or even in leafy suburbs.

Play out

There were stresses later on black children, too, who came to join their parents or were born in Britain. The 1979 National Dwelling and Housing Survey showed that while 3 per cent of white families shared an amenity, such as a bathroom, the figure was 9 per cent for West Indians; while 5 per cent of whites suffered from overcrowding, it was nearly 20 per cent for West Indians. This made it harder to break down barriers at school. How could you invite friends home to listen to records if your whole family lived in one room where the walls were so thin anyway that neighbours would complain about the noise? What black youths could do, of course, was meet on the street. This, too, could lead to problems.

In an interview in *Talking Blues* (1978) Handsworth's Reverend Ermal Kirby said:

> There are policemen who are, shall we say, over-eager, over-zealous, in carrying out their duties, so that they will pick on black youths for things which we would consider absolutely trivial. You cannot be seen talking to your friends for five minutes before a policeman is going to come along and tell you to move on. I think policemen are to some extent reflecting the attitudes and the feelings of the population, therefore they feel that they are being backed by society when they pick on blacks.

When Lord Scarman investigated the Brixton riots in 1981, he stated:

> Many young black people . . . feel a sense of frustration and deprivation. And living much of their lives on the streets, they are brought into contact with the police who appear to them as the visible symbols of the authority of a society which has failed to bring them its benefits or do them justice.

On 7 May 1976 Robert Relf of Leamington Spa was sent to prison after refusing to take down this sign. He told the judge that race relations people were 'hell-bent on handing over our country to the black man'.

> Stay away from Wilmslow if you're black. Chief Inspector Clinton told a recent parish meeting that such people were liable to be picked up for questioning: 'We don't have black people living in Wilmslow', he explained. 'It is obvious that they are strangers. There is nothing in Wilmslow to attract people from Moss Side except the houses.'
>
> *The Guardian*, 20 June 1985

11 Changing images

Blacks in early comics might be friendly, but were seldom smart.

Paul Robeson in *Sanders of the River*.

Seen from a distance

Before World War II, in the days before wide-spread car ownership made people more mobile, many whites who lived outside Britain's ports and big cities had never spoken to black people at first hand. What these whites knew about people with dark skins came from comics, magazines, books, tales told by friends and, increasingly, from films.

Can images on screen, in feature films or in TV commercials, affect the way we think and speak? Or influence us to find one thing more attractive than another? If so, in the early days of cinema, any whites who knew little about black people were likely to have their worst prejudices confirmed. The early films were made by whites for whites. Many films came from the USA, where racial segregation was rife.

Blacks were not shown in positions of authority over whites – and tiny, white, child star Shirley Temple could make the hugest black tremble. Unless they could do song-and-dance, women usually played plump, jolly cooks, while men were melon-eating, yes-sirring servants who rolled their eyes wildly at a clap of thunder. When Malcolm X first saw the smash-hit *Gone with the Wind* (1939), he 'felt like crawling under the rug'. Hattie Mc-Daniel, who won an Oscar for her part as a loyal 'mammy' in the film (the first Oscar awarded to a black) was not even invited to its all-white premiere.

Countless Westerns showed palefaces as superior to people with a darker skin. Not many showed a black cowboy, of whom there were so many – like scout Jim Beckwourth, Pony Express riders William Robinson and George Munroe, or Oklahoman Bill Picket, who became a rodeo star. Black actors were sometimes hired to play scantily-clad jungle-dwellers (as Paul Robeson was for the British-made *Sanders of the River*, 1935); but the only star allowed to shine in a Hollywood jungle was Tarzan: a white man.

The Trinidadian-born actor and playwright Errol John (1924–88) appeared in over 20 films, including *The African Queen* (1951) and *The Nun's Story* (1959), but his career was held back by his frequent refusal to play roles which he felt would demean him as a black.

New images on screen

When the US civil rights movement made headway, new films emerged starring faultless black heroes with talent, charm and even a good job: for example, Oscar-winning Sidney Poitier in *Guess who's coming to dinner?*, *In the Heat of the Night* and *To Sir, with Love* (all released in 1967) and Bill Cosby in *I spy* (also 1967). 'Integrated' blacks like this were seen by huge white audiences. Fewer whites saw films about blacks who had other aims in life than to be accepted by whites, such as *The Harder They Come* (1972) – starring Jimmy Cliff and shot in Kingston, with a reggae sound-track and a cast of actors speaking broad Jamaican patois – or *Handsworth Songs*, which

was made in Britain by the Black Audio Film Collective.

The old pictures of blacks were being challenged in other ways. Cinema and TV newsreels now showed footage of blacks in real-life positions of responsibility. Numerous colonies in the West Indies and Africa had won independence and elected black leaders. Gradually, the early images were being eroded. Eventually, there would even be some strong screen roles for black women, as Leicester-born Josette Simon showed in *Milk and Honey* (1989).

Community spirit

Afro-Caribbeans were not always welcome in 'white' pubs and clubs, so they had to establish their own clubs and social centres. These became the focus for community activities, from a game of dominoes to providing child care and education. The black community had already set up several newspapers before Trinidadian Claudia Jones (1915–64) came to Britain in 1958 and edited the radical *West Indian Gazette*. She also set to work to establish London's Carnival tradition.

State institutions like the National Gallery seemed unaware that black people existed. It was thus a step forward when the Africa Centre in Covent Garden was opened by President Kaunda of Zambia in 1962 and began to run a programme of films, conferences and poetry readings by black artists. Exhibitions were run by the Commonwealth Institute, too. All this highlighted the need for a bookshop offering a full range of black literature. In 1966 John La Rose and Sarah White opened New Beacon, first as a publishers, then as a bookshop, too. More shops followed – selling everything from tomes on history and detective stories to children's tales about Anansi Spider.

The Notting Hill Carnival

Carnivals began in the Eastern Caribbean after the abolition of slavery. They were a form of masquerading fun that mimicked white processions. The first Notting Hill Carnival took

Sidney Poitier, who grew up in the Bahamas, in a scene from *Buck and the Preacher* (1972) with his co-star Harry Belafonte – better known as a Top Ten vocalist with hits such as *Island in the Sun* (1957). 'I'm an average Joe Blow Negro', said Sidney Poitier in 1964. 'But as the cats say in my area, I'm out there wailing for us all'.

The Notting Hill Carnival usually has an atmosphere of easy-going fun, as shown here. But this mood was upset in 1976 after 1600 police turned up, instead of just 80 as the year before. If pickpocketing was the fear, some blacks felt the presence of so many police at 'our party' was an insult that destroyed the occasion. Tension had long existed, with the police criticised by black community leaders for 'harassment and brutality against sections of the youth'. Fighting broke out and 50 blacks were arrested.

Carnival provides a showcase for eye-catching craft skills, which blend ancient African traditions with a modern imagination and ingenuity. The black community takes great pride in this and hours of effort are devoted to it. As soon as one carnival ends, work begins on designs for the next.

place in 1958 and drew a crowd of about 7,000 people. The Carnival is now held every August, run by blacks. It is a chance to meet old friends, eat Trinidadian specialities, enjoy contests for steel bands and sharp-witted calypso singers, and display the black community's beautiful craft traditions. When Jamaican reggae music pounded out from the sound-systems in the mid-70s, ever greater numbers came. Leeds and other cities had Caribbean carnivals, too, but Notting Hill became Europe's largest street festival. It now lasts for two days and attracts over a million people.

Could do better

The school system in Britain's colonies in the Caribbean looked towards Britain and copied its school uniforms, exams and schoolbooks. So Afro-Caribbeans in Britain expected their children to fit in here easily and do well. They were very concerned when their children sometimes did not do as well as they had hoped. From the mid-1960s, certain that their children could do better if taught properly, the black community practised self-help. 'Supplementary schools' were organised at weekends to provide extra lessons. But what was going wrong?

In 1971, New Beacon published a study called *How the West Indian Child is Made Educationally Subnormal by the British School System*, by Bernard Coard. He identified two problems:

- Early tests which tended to grade pupils from immigrant families lower than others. These pupils were then put into classes for slow learners, and often reacted by switching off;

- The attitudes of white teachers.

In 1972 only 1.1 per cent of pupils in state schools were 'West Indians', but they made up 4.9 per cent of those at schools for the educationally sub-normal (ESN).

A study of secondary school exam results showed it was Afro-Caribbean boys, rather than girls, whose achievements were below those of whites and pupils of Asian origin. The cause, yet more inquiries suggested, was that:

- few schools had any black teachers, headteachers were even rarer, and many white teachers *expected* black immigrants' children to do badly;

Dominican born Patricia Scotland went to school in Britain and she remembers her careers teacher. 'She said I shouldn't set my sights too high. I had a Saturday job at a supermarket – and she thought I might become a supervisor there.' In fact, Patricia became a lawyer. At the age of 35, in 1991, she became Britain's first black woman Queen's Counsel

Ezz Witter helps to run the Mandela Centre in the Chapeltown district of Leeds (which was opened by Darcus Howe in 1984). His family came from Jamaica. In 1988, his schooldays now well behind him, Ezz could still remember a careers lesson he was given at school. 'All of the other youths in my class were white, but no brighter than I was. The teacher kept telling them to apply for a post in a bank. When he came to me, he asked if I'd thought of a factory job, engineering perhaps. Up to then, I hadn't been too aware of suffering discrimination.'

Winston Wilkinson (l.) and Ezz Witter (r.) are leaders at the Mandela Centre in Chapeltown, Leeds, where the activities include football, campaigns against drug abuse, and a supplementary school.

Until quite recently pictures of blacks in Britain tended to be exotic or strange and were seldom positive or flattering. It was almost impossible to buy a birthday card that showed a black having fun.

- white teachers knew little about black history, and lessons dealt only with whites' contributions to the world;
- teachers stopped young black children from using patois or Creole, which caused many to lose confidence – and made some shy, others aggressive;
- black pupils who were 'difficult' were sent to ESN schools too quickly.
- many black pupils came from deprived homes and black youths spent a lot of time out in the streets.

The debates went on. Does it matter what teachers expect of a pupil? How important is confidence? Should pupils learn standard English more quickly?

Images to look up to?

While the Department of Education recognised in 1977 that it was not suitable to gear lessons to 'the Imperial past', black parents still doubted whether what schools offered was right for a multi-cultural society. Some state schools offered lessons on 'the three S's' (saris, steel bands and samosas). But a few lessons on food, festivals or folklore said little about the role of black people in British history or modern society. The British Empire had once contained over 370 million blacks, and surely some must be worthy of study, as role models perhaps, by blacks and by whites together?

Afro-Caribbean parents criticised some school library books, such as editions of *Robinson Crusoe*, that showed blacks as inferior to whites, but left out the chapters which showed Crusoe as a slaveholder who was shipwrecked while seeking new slaves. It was realised that the phrases teachers used could affect children's ideas of themselves, too. Blacks in some cases were called 'natives', for example, but no whites anywhere ever were. Except in geography lessons, it could be hard to find a black face in a textbook. Youngsters often read *The*

Three Musketeers, but who ever told them that its author was the grandson of a black woman, whose surname he took?

Not that schools were different from the rest of society. In 1979, a selection of comics was analysed – in 3,384 drawings, there were only three black faces! Some parents were also concerned about the crude images of black people that were used in the advertising or packaging of goods such as jam. When they took their children to toy shops, they found golliwogs, which all looked alike, but otherwise all the toy figures were white. It could hurt, too, to see goods advertised as 'flesh-coloured'.

The image of blacks given in schools began to change. But the lead was coming from outside the classroom and the school gates – with the help of reggae and Rastafarianism – from blacks themselves, especially the youth.

Rasta and reggae

In the 1960s and 1970s, when a lot of young whites in Britain flirted with Eastern religions, gurus and marijuana, some Afro-Caribbeans, mainly young men, became interested in the ideas and customs of the Rastafarian movement.

Arising in Jamaica in the 1930s, it had many strands, including African history and rhythms and Biblical stories. As a style of life it could be religious or political or both. Some Rastamen saw no hope for themselves in a 'Babylon' dominated by whites and withdrew into a mystical world or spoke of 'returning' to Africa. Others were determined to stay put and stand up for their rights. At the heart of Rasta lay Ethiopia – its past, present and future.

To young Afro-Caribbeans who knew only how their forebears had knelt before white missionaries and a white monarch, it was refreshing to hear of an African state with a longer Christian tradition than England and a black royal family that claimed a line back to Menelik I, son of Solomon and Queen Makeda

In the 1980s anonymous artists added colour to some of the street signs in Liverpool 8. However, the colours that they used were not chosen at random. Far from it.

of Sheba. Ethiopia's ruler for almost half a century was Ras Tafari [Ras = prince] who became the 111th Emperor, Haile Selassie I, King of Kings in 1930 and was revered as if he were a god, the Lion of Judah (especially after his return to the throne in 1941 on the defeat of the invading Italians). Further age-old links to the Bible could be seen in an ancient black Jewish community, the Falashas, living in Ethiopia. The way many Rastas grew their hair was not intended as a revival of the style worn by the Cavaliers of Charles I: their long 'dreadlocks' had a Biblical basis, and the form was African. The striped woollen tams (hats) that they wore usually displayed the Ethiopian national colours of red, green and gold – often together with black.

A common link between Rastafarians was the importance they placed on Africa as their spiritual homeland. They accepted the view of Marcus Garvey, a Jamaican who campaigned for blacks from 1916 to 1925 in the USA:

66 If the white man has the idea of a white God, let him worship his God as he desires, but we shall worship him through the spectacles of Ethiopia. 99

What attracted many young people, however, black and white, was the beat of the reggae music that was associated with Rastas. And what drew the attention of the police, in Britain and the West Indies, was the use some Rastas made of cannabis (a drug known in the Caribbean by its Hindi name, ganja). Musical evidence of an interest in cannabis came in *Legalise it*, a reggae number by Peter Tosh.

Arrests on drugs charges, prison terms, the overthrow of Haile Selassie, the early death of top reggae stars like Bob Marley and other members of the Wailers, Peter Tosh and Carlton Barrett – all dealt blows to the Rasta movement. So did TV reports in the 1980s showing huge problems in Ethiopia. Nonetheless, in its most basic form, an assertion of heritage and equality, Rasta remained popular.

Just sounds?

While whites had long appreciated many black musical styles – gospel songs, the blues, jazz, ska, all with roots that go back to Africa – they had not always been aware of the feelings and the experience that gave birth to them. It was the same story with reggae. When reggae tracks from Jamaica hit the air-waves, teenagers in Britain took to the music without caring whether they could understand the lyrics, which often enough were not in standard English. Black youth gained access quickly. But how could whites understand the depth of feeling here unless they knew something of the history that had led to the present situation? Only gradually did they begin to realise that here were songs that:

- recalled the days of slavery;
- opposed the racism still facing black people;
- asserted solidarity with Africa;
- demanded change – now.

For raising awareness, reggae music proved to be an ideal vehicle; and Bob Marley – the son of a Jamaican woman and a white soldier from Liverpool – was its first superstar. Bob Marley and the Wailers entered the British charts in 1975 and their hits never lost their popularity. Their recordings included an anthem to ZANU guerilla fighters in their struggle for independence in Zimbabwe, which Marley was invited to perform in Harare as part of the independence celebrations in 1980.

Some typical lines from songs sung by Bob Marley and The Wailers:

'Every time I hear the crack of the whip,
My blood runs cold.
I remember on the slave ship
how they brutalized my very soul.'
from *Slave Driver*

'I and I build the cabin,
I and I plant the corn.
Didn't my people before me
slave for this country?
Now you look at we with scorn
And eat up all the corn.'
from *Crazy Baldhead*

'Them belly full, but we hungry.
A hungry mob is a angry mob.'
from *Them Belly Full*

'Now we know everything – we've got to rebel.
Somebody got to pay for the work we've done.
Rebel.'
from *Babylon System*

'If you know what life is worth,
You will look for yours on earth.'
from *Get up, Stand up for your Rights*

A stamp issued in Jamaica to honour Bob Marley (1945–82).

In the late 1980s, Benjamin Zephaniah became Britain's best known Rastafarian poet.

12 Not needed now?

The situation changes

From 1951 to 1964 Britain was governed by Conservatives. With their encouragement, at first there was a marked rise in the number of people coming from the Caribbean: over 20,000 a year in the late 1950s. The economy blossomed. In 1953 Britain exported more cars than France, Japan, West Germany and Italy together. In 1959 the country's slogan was 'You've never had it so good'.

By 1961, however, greater competition from rebuilt economies abroad led to a slowing down here; and Britain decided to join the European Economic Community or 'Common Market'. The first application failed, but it showed how Britain was turning away from its overseas ties.

This graph shows how many 'people with one or both parents born in the West Indies' came to live in Britain between 1939 and 1970. At first more men arrived, then more women. Between 1971 and 1973 some 14,000 left again, while there were only 9,000 new arrivants.

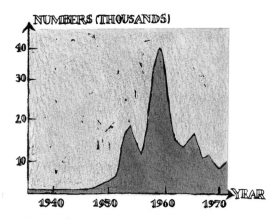

NUMBERS (THOUSANDS)

40
30
20
10

1940   1950   1960   1970   YEAR

In 1962 three key changes took place:

- the Conservative government passed a new law to limit immigration from the Commonwealth – this took away the right of many Commonwealth citizens with British passports to settle in Britain;
- Britain gave independence to its two largest West Indian colonies: Jamaica (where over half the West Indian immigrants came from) and Trinidad & Tobago;
- it became easier for West Indians to find work in the USA again.

The numbers coming to Britain from the Caribbean now dwindled and ever tighter laws kept immigration low.

Protective measures

In the House of Commons on 5 November 1954, Henry Hopkinson, the Minister of State for the Colonies, had said:

66 In a world in which restrictions on personal movement and immigration have increased, we can still take pride in the fact that a man can say *civis Britannicus sum* (I am a British citizen) whatever his colour may be, and we take pride in the fact that he wants to and can come to the Mother Country. 99

By 1962 that age was over. A new wind blew now. Whatever the exact wording of the 1962 law, or the stricter laws that came later, the idea was not to reduce immigration – it was not about numbers, few worried about the number of whites coming here – it was to keep out blacks. With this law, Ambalvaner Sivanandan of the Institute of Race Relations said:

66 Racialism was no longer a matter of free enterprise. It was nationalized. 99

At the same time, Parliament did now introduce various new laws to protect blacks who were already here. Step by step, between 1965 and 1976, it became unlawful to practise direct or indirect discrimination – on grounds of colour, race or ethnic or national origin – in advertisements, education and training, employment, housing, and in the provision of goods, facilities and services.

1962 law. Of all the candidates, Fenner Brockway, Labour MP for Eton and Slough, spoke out most strongly against racism. Patrick Gordon Walker – who was tipped to be Foreign Minister if Labour won the election – was a candidate in Smethwick. He faced a Tory opponent, Peter Griffiths, who was backed by a campaign using the slogan: 'If you want a nigger for a neighbour, vote Liberal or Labour'. How would voters react?

Griffiths was elected. The voters' message was clear. Although Labour won the general election overall, the 1962 Act was not repealed.

Not to be 'swamped'

To whites in Britain who wanted blacks to be sent 'home', Enoch Powell, the MP for Wolverhampton South-West, became a hero. As Minister for Health from 1960 to 1963 Powell had employed thousands of black workers from abroad. Now, from the mid-1960s to the early 1990s, he spoke of 'alien wedges in the heartland of the state' and warned of violence on a huge scale. His lurid speeches could bring him 100,000 letters of support, many from immigration officers and dockers. In April 1968, he said,

66 As I look ahead, I am filled with foreboding. Like the Roman, I seem to see the River Tiber foaming with much blood 99

After this speech Edward Heath, leader of the Conservatives, sacked Powell from his Shadow Cabinet. Seeing their champion treated in this way, some whites switched their support now to the National Front, an openly racist party, which was founded in 1966 and was growing in strength.

Edward Heath's successor, Margaret Thatcher, took this seriously. In a TV interview in January 1978, she said that British people were rather afraid that this country and the British character, which had 'done so much for democracy, for law, and done so much throughout the world' might be 'swamped by people with a different culture'. She said people had the right to be reassured about numbers, that neglect of the immigration issue was driving some people to support the National Front, and that 'we are not in politics to ignore people's worries but to deal with them'.

The Conservatives went on to win the next general election in 1979, and support for the National Front fell away.

Fenner Brockway's front door. It took some courage for whites to speak up in support of blacks' rights. Brockway's views lost him his seat in the House of Commons. In his *Diaries of a Cabinet Minister* (1975), Richard Crossman wrote: 'Ever since the Smethwick election it has been quite clear that immigration can be the greatest potential vote-loser for the Labour Party if we are seen to be permitting a flood of immigrants to come and blight the central areas in all our cities.'

The 1976 Race Relations Act also set up the Commission for Racial Equality (CRE) to watch out for discrimination and to promote good relations between groups.

These and later measures brought improvements for blacks in Britain. However, Britain's economic problems in the late 1960s and a rise in unemployment in the mid-1970s led to increased attacks upon blacks. Calls of 'Send them back home!' grew louder.

The majority rules

In 1958 Tom Driberg, Chairman of the Labour Party, said at the Trades Union Congress:

66 The real problem is not black skins, but white prejudice. 99

Whites who disagreed with him looked for politicians who understood their feelings.

In the run-up to the 1964 general election there was talk that Labour would repeal the

In modern times, as in the days of Wedderburn and Davidson, blacks have joined with whites on, for example, marches to highlight unemployment and on picket lines during an industrial strike.

Problems at work

The arrivals from the Caribbean came to Britain to work. On average, they were healthier and younger than whites (a growing number of whom were pensioners). By 1971 only 77 per cent of white men were 'in work or seeking work', compared with 91 per cent of black men. With women the situation was similar – a higher proportion of blacks worked.

Then, in the 1970s, there was an oil crisis and a recession. According to the *Department of Employment Gazette* (1980), from 1973 to 1980 the number of people out of work doubled – but black unemployment went up fourfold. Racism no doubt played a part in this; and in *A portrait of English racism* (1973), Ann Dummett quoted an employer who asked:

❝Why is it wrong for me to refuse to have any of these people in my firm when the Government is refusing to have them come into the country?❞

The full picture was more complex. Rising unemployment hit blacks harder than whites, on the whole, because:

- more blacks were of working age;
- the jobs or industries that employed the most blacks were not as secure as those that employed more whites;

- having been low-paid when they were in work, blacks were unlikely to have much in the way of savings;
- employers might turn down applicants from an address in, say, Liverpool 8;
- blacks risked trouble if they tried to look for lodgings and work in areas where whites did not welcome black people.

Getting a true picture

Unemployment hit young blacks hardest of all. By 1982, one survey found, 60 per cent of Afro-Caribbeans in the 16 to 20 age group were without work. In 1983 Leon Brittan, the Home Secretary, said:

❝It is a hard fact that ethnic minorities suffer disproportionately from unemployment; there is incontrovertible research evidence to back up individual experience of discrimination in recruitment or selection.❞

In *Black and White Britain* (1984) Colin Brown presented research confirming this statement. 5,000 black people of Asian and West Indian origin had been interviewed and also over 2,000 white people. When asked if there were employers who would refuse a job to a person because of their race or colour, more than two-thirds, even of whites, replied 'yes'. The survey found that a large proportion of 'West Indians' were skilled manual workers. Whites were more often non-manual workers – and they earned more. In manufacturing industry, nearly one in three white men had a non-manual job: among 'West Indian' men it was one in twenty. Trade union membership was higher among 'West Indians' than whites, both among men and women. 'West Indians' were more often in jobs that were likely to vanish if new technology was introduced.

Another survey, *British Social Attitudes, the 1984 Report* found that 90 per cent of those interviewed felt Britain was a racially-prejudiced society, and about 60 per cent thought discrimination flourished.

The Code of Practice

To fight injustice in the workplace, the Commission for Racial Equality devised a Code of Practice. This code came into force in 1984 and was approved by most of the 300 black groups the Commission had consulted, as well as by trade unions, the Confederation of British Industry (representing employers) and

64

by Parliament. It was a yardstick by which to measure what was going on. Some firms were still discriminating in ways that had been made unlawful, and the Code made it easier to spot them.

Traditional ways of doing things had excluded blacks from some firms. If there was a job going, those who already worked there told their friends or relatives about it. As a result, a company's entire workforce could be whites, even in areas where most people were black – and an employer could truthfully say, 'Yes, but no blacks ever apply'. With the help of the Code, some employers now realised for the first time that there were newspapers such as the *Caribbean Times* or *The Voice* where they could advertise.

Awkward questions

How can we tell whether an individual black's experience of discrimination is unusual or part of a wider pattern? Some organisations, such as the Army, kept no records of recruitment from the black community or of how many blacks were promoted, claiming simply that everyone was treated equally. However, no data could be produced to support this claim – while the testimony of blacks such as ex-Corporal Sonny Freeman (who never took part in Trooping the Colour) as well as a 1989 book by two white former cavalry officers, *A New Model Army*, argued that the Army's claim was false. To clarify the situation, an all-party House of Commons committee has demanded ethnic monitoring in the armed forces.

Parliament also decided that the 1991 census of Britain's population would ask people to which ethnic group they belonged. This would show whether blacks were under-represented as, say, head teachers (in 1989 there were fewer than 20 in the whole country) or show whether it was odd that a 1989 survey of city centre shops in Liverpool found only 15 blacks among the 981 counter staff.

Many whites were nonetheless wary of questions about ethnic origin and some blacks recalled the words of a junior Government minister, Alan Clark, who in 1983 had said:

66 You mean to say that they don't want us collecting their names and addresses because they're afraid we're going to hand them over to the Immigration Service so they can send them all back to Bongo-Bongo land? 99

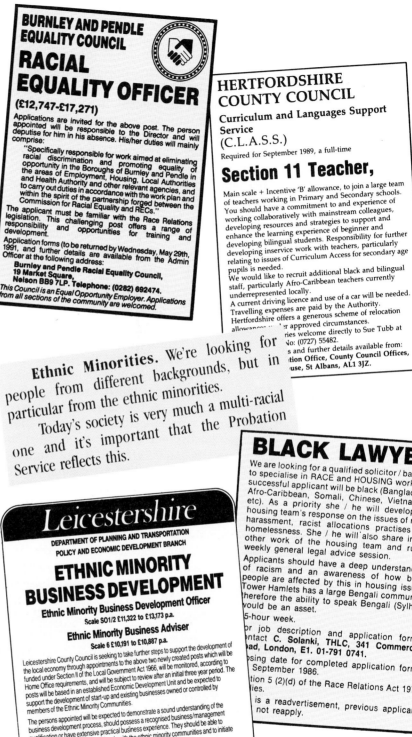

BURNLEY AND PENDLE EQUALITY COUNCIL

RACIAL EQUALITY OFFICER

(£12,747–£17,271)

Applications are invited for the above post. The person appointed will be responsible to the Director and will deputise for him in his absence. His/her duties will mainly comprise:

"Specifically responsible for work aimed at eliminating racial discrimination and promoting equality of opportunity in the Boroughs of Burnley and Pendle in the areas of Employment, Housing, Local Authorities and Health Authority and other relevant agencies, and to carry out duties in accordance with the work plan and within the spirit of the partnership forged between the Commission for Racial Equality and RECs."

The applicant must be familiar with the Race Relations legislation. This challenging post offers a range of responsibility and opportunities for training and development.

Application forms (to be returned by Wednesday, May 29th, 1991, and further details are available from the Admin Officer at the following address:

Burnley and Pendle Racial Equality Council,
19 Market Square,
Nelson BB9 7LP. Telephone: (0282) 692474.

This Council is an Equal Opportunity Employer. Applications from all sections of the community are welcomed.

HERTFORDSHIRE COUNTY COUNCIL

Curriculum and Languages Support Service
(C.L.A.S.S.)

Required for September 1989, a full-time

Section 11 Teacher,

Main scale + Incentive 'B' allowance, to join a large team of teachers working in Primary and Secondary schools. You should have a commitment to and experience of working collaboratively with mainstream colleagues, developing resources and strategies to support and enhance the learning experience of beginner and developing bilingual students. Responsibility for further developing inservice work with teachers, particularly relating to issues of Curriculum Access for secondary age pupils is needed.

We would like to recruit additional black and bilingual staff, particularly Afro-Caribbean teachers currently underrepresented locally.

A current driving licence and use of a car will be needed. Travelling expenses are paid by the Authority.

Hertfordshire offers a generous scheme of relocation allowances ... for approved circumstances.

... ries welcome directly to Sue Tubb at ... No: (0727) 55482.

... s and further details available from: ...tion Office, County Council Offices, ...use, St Albans, AL1 3JZ.

Ethnic Minorities. We're looking for people from different backgrounds, but in particular from the ethnic minorities. Today's society is very much a multi-racial one and it's important that the Probation Service reflects this.

Leicestershire
DEPARTMENT OF PLANNING AND TRANSPORTATION
POLICY AND ECONOMIC DEVELOPMENT BRANCH

ETHNIC MINORITY BUSINESS DEVELOPMENT

Ethnic Minority Business Development Officer
Scale SO1/2 £11,322 to £13,173 p.a.

Ethnic Minority Business Adviser
Scale 6 £10,191 to £10,887 p.a.

Leicestershire County Council is seeking to take further steps to support the development of the local economy through appointments to the above two newly created posts which will be funded under Section II of the Local Government Act 1966, will be monitored, according to the Home Office requirements, and will be subject to review after an initial three year period. The posts will be based in an established Economic Development Unit and be expected to support the development of start-up and existing businesses owned or controlled by members of the Ethnic Minority Communities.

The persons appointed will be expected to demonstrate a sound understanding of the business development process, should possess a recognised business/management qualification or have extensive practical business experience. They should be able to demonstrate the ability to work closely with the ethnic minority communities and to initiate actions to meet identified needs.

Because the officers will be dealing almost exclusively with persons of either Afro-Caribbean or Asian origin, a working knowledge of the cultures served is essential. Indeed Afro-Caribbeans and Asians are under represented in this area of the Council's work and are therefore positively encouraged to apply.

Relocation expenses up to £2,460 payable in appropriate circumstances. Temporary housing could be available.

For further information contact the Economic Development Officer, David Dugdale, on Leicester (0533) 317886.

Application forms and further details obtainable by telephoning Leicester (0533) 316613, or by writing to the Director of Planning and Transportation, County Hall, Leicester LE3 8RJ.

Closing date Friday 5th February 1988.

EQUAL OPPORTUNITIES POLICY: Applications are welcome from people regardless of their race, ethnic origin, religion, sex, marital status or disability; disabled applicants will be guaranteed an interview if suitably qualified and/or experienced, and supported by a recognised agency e.g. a D.R.O.

BLACK LAWYER

We are looking for a qualified solicitor / barrister to specialise in RACE and HOUSING work. The successful applicant will be black (Bangladeshi, Afro-Caribbean, Somali, Chinese, Vietnamese etc). As a priority she / he will develop the housing team's response on the issues of racial harassment, racist allocations practises and homelessness. She / he will also share in the other work of the housing team and run a weekly general legal advice session.

Applicants should have a deep understanding of racism and an awareness of how black people are affected by this in housing issues. Tower Hamlets has a large Bengali community, therefore the ability to speak Bengali (Sylheti) would be an asset.

...5-hour week.

...r job description and application forms, ...ntact C. Solanki, THLC, 341 Commercial ...ad, London, E1. 01-791 0741.

...sing date for completed application forms ... September 1986.

...tion 5 (2)(d) of the Race Relations Act 1976 ...ies.

...is a readvertisement, previous applicant ...not reapply.

New-style job advertisements encouraged black applicants to apply.

Violence and book burning

There have been many instances of whites using physical violence on Britain's visible minorities. These have included attacks on homes, physical assault, verbal abuse and other forms of harassment. In 1958 London's black community was alarmed by the murder of a Jamaican-born carpenter, Kelso Cochrane, which remained unsolved. In that same year, after 'race riots' in the Midlands had hit the headlines, there was fighting in London's Notting Hill. This led to nine white youths being sent to prison. The judge, Lord Justice Salmon, said they had filled the nation with disgust:

66 Everyone, irrespective of the colour of their skin, is entitled to walk through our streets with heads erect and free from fear. 99

Instead of easing, the attacks grew worse. Some whites, chiefly young men, organised themselves in military-style bodies that used symbols and salutes like those of Hitler's Nazis. They distributed pamphlets attacking black people and Jews. In the years that followed, anti-racists came together to combat these groups. Racists and anti-racists clashed on numerous occasions. In 1979 the National Front (NF) held an election meeting at the Town Hall in Southall, London. About 2700 police with dogs and horses were there to protect the civil rights of NF supporters from the anti-racists who had gathered to protest. In the scuffles that followed there were 345 arrests, and over 160 people were injured. Some police officers used unauthorised batons, and Blair Peach, a white man demonstrating against the NF was killed by a blow on the head. (In 1989 the police paid £75,000 compensation for this, without admitting responsibility).

Not enough help?

In addition to thousands of attacks on black people, there were attacks on bookshops that specialised in black literature. Centerprise bookshop in Hackney was fire-bombed in 1977 and attacked again in 1985. Sprayed slogans claimed this as the work of the British National Party. Bogle-L'Ouverture (see page 38) was vandalised several times. The shop's owners, the Huntleys, felt that the police were not doing enough to catch the culprits. Increasingly, young blacks did not see the police as their protectors. If people of Asian origin suffered most, Afro-Caribbeans were not spared. At a railway station in Ilford in 1985, ticket-collector Peter Burns was taunted by some white youths, then his eye was pierced with a metal stake. He died.

Power of music

What pop stars, TV stars or sports personalities say, eat or wear not only interests their fans but can influence them. Thus, when black singers drew on their personal experience to sing

In 1981 in New Cross, London, 13 black people at a party died when the house caught fire. There was a history of arson attacks against the local black community. Was this arson, too? Some blacks felt that the police were not interested in finding out the truth. In a demonstration that Trinidadian-born Darcus Howe helped to organise, over 15,000 marched through London to draw attention to the need for action.

about what it means to be black in a society dominated by whites – or spoke about their lives in interviews or comments made on stage – they had a chance to bring home to their white fans what racism meant. They could speak to other blacks, too, and tell the story of the people through song. If state schools taught little about black history and culture, singers were able to act as a 'supplementary school'. Jamaican-born Stokely Carmichael, a radical black rights campaigner in the USA, said in 1970:

66 Malcolm X says that of all studies none rewards our research better than history. We must understand our history. 99

In 1983 Gary Byrd's 'rap' or rhythmical narration, *The Crown*, on pride in black heritage, and anti-drugs, climbed the US charts and shot to Number 6 in Britain. 'Professor' Byrd sang of the pyramids and the sphinx and of black achievers from 'King Tut' to Harriet Tubman, Jackie Robinson, Mohammed Ali, Julius Irving and writers Gwendolyn Brooks, Langston Hughes and Alex Haley:

66 I do recall so very well, when I was just a little boy, I used to hurry home from school, I used to always feel so blue, because there was no mention – in the books we read – about our heritage . . . And then one day, from someone old, I heard a story never told, of all the kingdoms of my people, and how they fought for freedom, all about the many things we have unto the world contributed . . . 99

Black and white together

In 1976 the black community had cause for alarm when several white pop stars aired unsympathetic views. In response, other pop stars put on gigs organised under the motto 'Rock against Racism' (RAR), starting at Hackney town hall. As Wayne Minter, a RAR organiser, recalled:

66 In 1976 the National Front were growing in Hackney and at the same time in that year Eric Clapton and David Bowie and Rod Stewart came up with some fairly racist comments. Eric Clapton said [at the Birmingham Odeon] that . . . Enoch Powell was right that all the blacks and Asians should be sent back. 99

New pop groups emerged, with names and songs that proclaimed 'white power' and referred to Nazi ideas. On through the 1980s, the 'Blood and Honour' groups won themselves fans; but they were far fewer than the myriads drawn by stars, both white and black, who came out publicly in support of a multiracial society.

From the mid-1980s issues on other continents brought a joint response once again, including relief aid for Africa. In 1988 a huge open-air, anti-apartheid concert celebrated Nelson Mandela's 70th birthday and in 1990 another concert celebrated his release from prison in South Africa. On television numerous stars helped to raise funds after Hurricane Gilbert struck Jamaica. In 1989, when Montserrat suffered terribly from a similar storm (most of the tiny island's 12,000 inhabitants losing their homes) black and white musicians again joined forces to release the fund-raising album, *After the hurricane*. When a team of cricketers, led by England's ex-captain Mike Gatting, wanted to play in South Africa in the winter of 1989–90, despite that country's racist practice of apartheid, some musicians joined figures from the black community, such as trade union leader Bill Morris, in an appeal to the players not to go. Politics came into sport, just as it did with music.

If regular radio stations chose not to play a 'political' track, increasingly blacks tuned in to their own pirate or independent radio stations

13 Trouble with the law

Tension

With all the attacks upon them, British blacks needed the police on their side. Instead, too often, they ran into police officers who added to their problems. Black people, especially the youth, were frequently stopped and searched by the police. Special 'sus laws' allowed the police to stop people if they suspected a crime. But was 'sus' used to harass blacks? In *Shattering Illusions* (1986) Trinidadian-born Trevor Carter wrote:

66 In 1975, out of 18,907 stop and searches in Greater London, 14,000 were in Lambeth and Lewisham alone, over a two-month period. This assault on two of London's biggest black communities resulted in just 403 arrests. 99

The manner in which the police treated blacks often caused offence. Even if innocent of any crime when stopped, a youth might become 'uppity' if provoked by racist remarks – and that might lead to arrest and an appearance in court on a charge of obstructing or assaulting a police officer. In court (usually in front of a white judge) those with steady jobs might be given a second chance. But many blacks found themselves in prison. In 1988, Vivien Stern, director of the National Association for the Care and Resettlement of Offenders, said:

At the end of last year Judge Suckling QC dismissed charges of assault against Derek Donaldson, a musician with the group Sons of Jah, which arose out of police officers attempting to search Mr Donaldson. Judge Suckling … noted that the officers had given evidence that *anyone* in the Notting Hill Gate area is suspected of being in possession of a controlled drug and stated that 'what the officers said implies the police are misusing their powers on a wide scale'.
Civil Liberty, September 1985

A schoolboy who has been remanded in custody for a month accused of stealing 84p was released on bail last night after his lawyers appealed to a High Court judge. There was a storm of protest among the black community in Walsall, West Midlands, when magistrates remanded the 15-year-old Afro-Caribbean boy in custody last month after certifying him to be of unruly character. Walsall social services department told the magistrates the boy had never been in trouble with the police and they did not regard him as unruly. The boy's solicitor said last night: 'The boy feels he has been victimised because he is black'.
The Guardian, 22 April 1988

66 The evidence strongly indicates that black people are unfairly treated by our criminal justice system. The figures do not show that they are more prone to crime than white people but they do suggest that black people who offend are twice as likely to be sent to prison. 99

In 1990, having studied the evidence, Roy Hattersley, MP, the Shadow Home Secretary, said that Britain's criminal justice system showed 'an alarming degree of prejudice, both institutional and overt'. He said;

66 Black defendants are consistently sentenced to prison in cases which would not produce a prison sentence for a white offender. Overall, young people from the ethnic minorities are given sentences of imprisonment almost twice as frequently as their white counterparts and they are likely to be given longer sentences. 99

Even in prison, blacks hoped in vain for equal treatment. For example, as Sir James Hennessy (who was H.M. Chief Inspector of Prisons from 1982 to 1987) has pointed out,

An unfair cop, cries rally car owner

By Paul Brown

BARRY COY, a professional ice hockey player, has made a formal complaint of harassment against Merseyside police after being stopped more than 100 times since he bought a high-performance rally car in January.

Mr Coy, aged 20, says that police apparently cannot believe that a young West Indian can afford a £4,000 car.

He had sometimes been stopped as many as five times in one evening, and has been arrested on suspicion of stealing the car.

Despite all the police checks he has not been charged with any offence.

"At first I just laughed it off and the police made a joke when they realised they had stopped me before, but now I want it to stop," he said.

"I drive 50 miles to train at weekends and come back quite late. I live in a respectable neighbourhood in Formby and I keep getting followed home and questioned. It is not nice for my neighbours.

"It gets to the point where I can never guarantee to be anywhere on time because I know I will be held up by the police at least once."

Mr Coy has temporarily stopped driving and gets fellow ice hockey players to pick him up. His Ford Escort RS 2000 is in his garage, and he plans to sell it and buy a less conspicuous car.

He has an English mother and Jamaican father, but says he looks West Indian.

At one time he has had 14 police officers surrounding his house in the belief that he and his friends had stolen their cars.

Merseyside police said it was investigating a complaint of racial harrassment made by Mr Coy's solicitor, Valerie Limont. She said: "The police don't seem to think that a coloured person can make it on his own. Whenever they see Barry in his car they presume he's stolen it."

---

all the favourite jobs – such as kitchen work and hospital or reception duties – tended to be allocated to white prisoners.

An explosion

The illegal use of drugs within the black community was one reason for police searches. Yet blacks felt that many operations were aggressive and accompanied by racist abuse. Off the streets, black meeting places were raided repeatedly, often by large numbers of police. The Mangrove restaurant in Notting Hill drew in young people from all over London. In 1970, after the third raid in a year, a crowd of them demonstrated and fought with police. Journalist Darcus Howe was one of those put on trial after this, but not convicted. He said:

66 The Judge says he has 35 years of legal experience. Well, I have 400 years of colonial experience. 99

There were more clashes after raids at other clubs. From a police viewpoint, one can guess what success they would have if they raided a real cocaine den in small numbers and were awfully polite about it – or what might happen if they said no premises would ever be raided twice in the same year! Even if it were true that tobacco killed 100,000 a year, causing more harm than 'ganja', could the police ignore the laws which made it their duty to seek out cannabis? Some people, a judge included, felt cannabis should be legalised. Others, knowing a lack of resources made police select what to investigate, felt it better they should catch those who committed racist attacks.

More small-scale clashes, for example, in Leeds in 1975 and at the Notting Hill Carnival in 1976, added to the tension. In 1978 Pastor Blisset of the Bethel Church of God Fellowship in Handsworth warned:

66 The youths in Birmingham are like a time bomb, and sooner or later there is going to be an explosion. I hope to God that the eyes of the Government could be opened to this. 99

In fact it was in the St Paul's area of Bristol in April 1980 that the first 'explosion' occurred, when a black cafe owner was taken to a police car in handcuffs. Bristol had seen nothing like it since the riots of 1831 (see page 35). The police raid on the Black and White Cafe could

The *Guardian*, 24 August 1982.

A protest march through London.

Brixton, April 1981

be justified, for some 'ganja' was found as well as illicit alcohol. Blacks watching the raid, however, felt that the behaviour of the police was heavy-handed. They were angry. In the narrow streets around the cafe the crowd swelled to 2,000. If their anger was justified, their actions now were not. In the violence that followed, police officers were injured, dozens of police cars damaged or destroyed, and shops looted or set on fire.

Of the 134 people arrested, 11 blacks and one white were charged with rioting. At the trial, which ended in March 1981, none was found guilty of this. There was some dispute over what a 'riot' was exactly. As if to make the issue clear, a few days later in Brixton fresh violence erupted ...

The Scarman Report

After the events in Brixton during the weekend of 10–12 April 1981, the Home Secretary asked Lord Scarman, a senior judge (a white, like all his colleagues), to find out what had happened. His report spoke of scenes of:

> Where deprivation and frustration exist on the scale to be found among the young black people of Brixton, the probability of disorder must, therefore, be strong.
> *The Scarman Report*, 1981.

❝(violence and disorder) the like of which had not previously been seen in this century in Britain. In the centre of Brixton, a few hundred young people – most, but not all of them, black – attacked the police on the streets with stones, bricks, iron bars and petrol bombs ... Moreover, many of them, it is clear, believe, with justification that violence, though wrong, is a very effective means of protest.❞

Lord Scarman found that the events had 'originated spontaneously. There was no pre-meditation or plan. They quickly became a riot, the common purpose of the crowds being to attack the police'. It all followed a police operation known to the police as Swamp 81, 'an unfortunate name', the judge said. Swamp 81 was an intensive operation that had been running for a week. Ten squads, 112 officers in all, patrolled certain areas of Lambeth every day between 2 p.m. and 11 p.m. Out of a total of 943 'stops', 75 charges resulted, some of which were for obstructing the police during the operation. The *Scarman Report* stated:

❝One of the most serious developments in recent years has been the way in which the older generation of black people in Brixton has come to share the belief of the younger generation that the police routinely harass and ill-treat black youngsters.❞

After meeting witnesses and examining evidence, Lord Scarman concluded that unemployment was a major factor at the root of the disorders here and in other inner-city areas. In Brixton the rate of unemployment among black males under 19 was 55 per cent.

❝In a materialistic society, the relative ... deprivation it entails is keenly felt, and idleness gives time for resentment and envy to grow. Many of these difficulties face white as well as black youngsters, but it is clear that they bear particularly heavy on young blacks [who] face the burden of discrimination.❞

For the immediate future, Lord Scarman recommended that:

- schools offer a broad education in the humanities to help the various ethnic groups (including the 'host community') to understand each other's background and culture;
- positive action [be taken]. In this respect the ethnic minorities can be compared with any

other group with special needs, 'such as the elderly or one-parent families';

● an 'ethnic question' be included in the next census of the UK population, to back up 'positive action';

● every possible step be taken to prevent and to root out racially prejudiced attitudes in the police services.

Riots, looting, death

Following the riots in Brixton in April 1981, there came twelve months of similar incidents in other inner-city areas – including Toxteth, Moss Side, Handsworth, Wolverhampton, Leicester and Bradford. In September 1985 the media spotlight fell on Handsworth again, when blacks took part in more riots and looting after a Rastafarian motorist had been questioned by police about his tax disc. Here, the media quite rightly stressed the horror of a shop fire during the riot in which two Asian men died (a crime for which, later, two white youths were charged).

At the end of September 1985 armed police burst into a home in Brixton. As they entered, Inspector Douglas Lovelock shot the startled occupant, Mrs Cherry Groce, leaving her paralysed. The police were searching for her son, who was believed to be armed, but he was not, in fact, at the house and no longer lived there.

In London again, only a week later, a young black man called Floyd Jarrett was arrested because the tax disc on his car had expired. While he was held in custody, police entered the home of his mother Mrs Cynthia Jarrett on the Broadwater Farm estate in Tottenham, searching for anything he might have stolen. During the search she was knocked over by a police officer and died of a heart attack. To the arrested man, his brother Michael, and to others in the black community, it was unacceptable that an expired tax disc could prompt such a chain of events.

In Brixton and in Tottenham blacks were outraged by these police actions. After demonstrations, came riots. Cars and buildings were set on fire, shops were looted, fire-fighters and police came under attack, hundreds of people were injured. The most serious casualty was PC Keith Blakelock, a policeman who was brutally murdered by a crowd of black youths at Broadwater Farm. While hunting for his killers, in the biggest investigation in the history of the Metropolitan Police, some policemen used dubious methods. Two 'confessions' they obtained were termed 'high fantasy' by the judge and thrown out of court. Many who already mistrusted the police and the courts wondered whether the three blacks who were finally convicted of the murder were not, in fact, the guilty ones.

On 11 November 1985 thousands of people joined a protest march to Hyde Park, led by Mrs Groce's mother and her solicitor, Paul Boateng.

Upper Parliament Street, Toxteth, 1981.

24-year-old Clinton McCurbin had been suspected of using a stolen credit card; his death in 1987 by asphyxiation (at the hands of arresting police officers not trained in the latest restraint techniques, it was explained) brought 500 into the streets of Wolverhampton for the funeral. By now several blacks had died while held in custody.

In October 1985, there were anti-police riots in Toxteth again. In the summer of 1987 shops in the Chapeltown area of Leeds were petrol bombed. The rioters included Afro-Caribbeans, Asians and whites. *The Times* of 24 July reported that it had all begun when police arrested a black youth aged 17 after a gang allegedly kicked their car. After the arrest police were stoned and a taxi was hijacked and set alight. The Chief Constable of West Yorkshire said he had sympathy with the plight of young, unemployed blacks but he would not be soft on crime or criminals. Chapeltown, the *Times'* report added, 'still has housing problems. Unemployment among black youngsters runs at about 50 per cent'.

Why not join the force?

Would relations between the police and the black community improve if blacks joined the police force?

London's Metropolitan Police recruited its first black officer in 1966. In 1986 Douglas Hogg, MP, Under-Secretary of State at the Home Office, said:

66 The police force in this country is a citizen's police force. It must not be imposed upon the community but should be representative of the community it serves. We all know that at present it is not. The latest figures show that less than seven police officers out of every 1,000 come from a black or Asian background; at the end of July 1986 there were 844. We are making progress but it is slow. 99

Black youths were not keen to apply. If they did – according to two studies carried out in 1984 with the backing of police in London and South Yorkshire – they faced racism at the hands of their white colleagues; and racist language between officers was 'on the whole expected, accepted and even fashionable'. When police misconduct was punished, this seemed to happen very slowly. The *Daily Mirror*, of 17 July 1987, noted:

66 A gang of police bullies who savagely beat up innocent schoolboys, then lied for four years to save their skins, were jailed for more than 16 years [in total] yesterday. The brutal officers leapt from a Transit van code-named November 33 and waded into the boys for a 'laugh' as the youngsters walked home from a fair in Holloway, North London, on 6 August, 1983. The boys, aged from 13 to 16, were kneed, kicked, punched and beaten with truncheons. 99

Outside the court Baltimore Ranger, who was aged 16 at the time of the crime and given two cut eyes and a broken nose, called the 18-month sentence on one officer a 'joke'. He said: 'It does not renew the confidence of the youth in the street'.

A pointed editorial in the *Caribbean Times*, 25 November 1988, said:

66 We would not deny that there are perfectly concrete areas where the police and the local community in Liverpool 8 could usefully cooperate. One such example is the proliferation in dealing in hard drugs in the area – something that is absolutely opposed by the vast majority from all sections in the community. [But] what is standing in the way is the attitude of the force. 99

14 The road ahead

Thoughts along the way

Is it not strange to think that they who ought to be considered as the most learned and civilised people in the world, that they should carry on a traffic of the most barbarous cruelty and injustice, and that many are become so dissolute as to think slavery, robbery and murder no crime?

Ottobah Cugoano, 1787

Raphael painted, Luther preached, Corneille wrote, and Milton sang; and through it all, for four hundred years, the dark captives wound to the sea amid the bleaching bones of the dead; for four hundred years the sharks followed the scurrying ships; for four hundred years Ethiopia stretched forth her hands unto God.

W. E. B. DuBois, 1903

Black men, you were once great; you shall be great again.

Marcus Garvey, 1923

The blacks will know as friends only those whites who are fighting in the ranks beside them. And whites will be there.

C. L. R. James, 1938

'The products of the Empire, sold abroad for dollars, have been paying for our food. Only the Empire has kept us, since the war, from disaster. British production has not risen fast enough.'

Enoch Powell, MP, 17 October 1951

Our possessions of the West Indies, like that of India, ... gave us the strength, the support, but especially the capital, the wealth, which enabled us to come through the great struggle of the Napoleonic Wars, and enabled us not only to acquire this worldwide appendage of possessions we have, but also to lay the foundation of that commercial and financial leadership which, when the world was young, when everything outside Europe was undeveloped, enabled us to make our great position in the world.

Winston Churchill, 1956

Before what?

In 1973 a Member of Parliament, Joan Lestor, reported this conversation between a white woman and a black girl.
Woman: Where are you from, dear?
Girl: I'm from Battersea.
Woman: No, where were you born?
Girl: I was born in Wolverhampton.
Woman: No, dear, I mean before that.

But a captive is one who is resisting that situation. At every moment he is engaged in working and plotting against it. You can hear it still in the songs of Jimmy Cliff and Bob Marley.

Earl Lovelace, 1982

The loss of our mother is great but we cannot sit back because she is gone. I think my mother's generation came to this country to pave the way for us, but they didn't quite succeed. Not because they didn't try. But where they didn't succeed we will have to succeed.

Michael Jarrett, Tottenham, 1985

Black people do not want to become more like white Britons. Black people want to maintain their own identities. The cause of 'the problem' is not blacks, is not 'racial disadvantage', but is white racism.

Clifford Boam, the National Association of Community Relations Councils, 1983

In *The struggle for black arts in Britain* (1985) Kwesi Owusu wrote;
'There are some museums in the West which have accumulated so many artefacts originally looted from their colonies that they do not even have the space to exhibit them.'

Black British youths are beginning to equate to the dispossessed African youths they see on television fighting the racial oppression of apartheid. They are daily faced with having to live in poor housing with no future hope or job prospects, leading lives of despair, frustration and hopelessness. At the turn of this century, apartheid in South Africa will have been assigned to the rubbish bin of history. Will England have black townships still burning?

Paul Stephenson, Bristol West Indian Parents and Friends Association, 1985

Some of the signposts along Britain's roads point to the history of Britain's blacks.

'Goree' is by the docks in Liverpool. According to *Liverpool Street Names* (1981) by T. Lloyd-Jones, it was named after the island off west Africa, where slaves were gathered together for shipment to the plantations.

'Jamaica Street' is in docklands on the edge of Liverpool 8, the scene of riots in 1981. It is cut in two by 'New Bird Street', named after Joseph Bird, a slave trader who was Mayor of Liverpool in 1746.

Into people's homes

In the early days of British television, black people were seldom seen on screen unless they could box, sing or play an instrument. They did not star in panel games; and calypsos sung by Cy Grant were less pointed than those sung in Trinidad by the Mighty Sparrow. Apart from the pioneering black women in day-time programmes for the very young, such as Floella Benjamin, the 'blacks' screened most often were probably the white men wearing black-face make-up in the *Black and White Minstrel Show*, which ran from 1958 to 1978. If comedians such as Lancashire chappie Charlie Williams appeared, jokes against 'darkies' were expected from them.

From the late 1960s black people were

Shirley Bassey, a singer from Cardiff's 'Tiger Bay' area, earned her own TV show in the 1960s. Beginning with *Banana Boat Song* in 1957, her hits found their way into the Top Ten until 1973.

Lenny Henry, comedian par exellence, born in Dudley in 1958, with Britain's top heavyweight boxer of the 1980s, Frank Bruno, MBE. 'If you want to make a point,' Henry once said, 'make a joke about it. So people laugh and then they think.' Do you know what he means?

spoken of as 'wogs' and 'coons' in *Till death do us part*, a popular comedy series that got people talking about race – but not always positively. ITV's *Love thy Neighbour* appeared in 1972 with roles for two blacks, but poor ratings killed it.

After Sidney Poitier's success on the wide screen as policeman Virgil Tibbs in *In the Heat of the Night* (1967), a wave of new US TV films appeared with a black cop as part of a team. If the stories were worlds away from reality, at least they now offered black heroes, from Bill Cosby in *I spy* to Philip Michael Thomas as Tubbs in *Miami Vice* 20 years later.

Behind the scenes in 1981 Trinidadian-born Jocelyn Barrow, OBE, was made a BBC governor and a black showcase series, *Ebony*, emerged. When Channel 4 opened, wider issues and fresh comedy broke out in an alternative show, *Black on Black*. From 1984 Lenny Henry had a regular show of his own. Here, jokes about 'darkies' were faded out. A black audience could laugh without crying at the same time. If no blacks were to be seen in early TV soap operas, like *Coronation Street*, actors such as Judith Jacob and Vince Johnson did find their way into a more modern soap opera, *EastEnders*. Blacks were working behind cameras, too. Previously, as newscaster Zeinab Badawi put it, the 'Third World' tended to be shown only 'if there was a war, coup or famine'. In the later 1980s programme-makers such as Darcus Howe homed in on the varied reality of black people's lives at home and abroad with *Bandung File*.

Part of the team

Black British sportsmen and women have brought enormous pleasure to fans, have added to Britain's successes in the international arena, and have often been a target of abuse. On 21 December 1984 the *Daily Mail* reported:

66 Noel Blake resumed training with his Portsmouth club after suffering racist abuse from home fans the previous Saturday. Brendan Batson, assistant secretary of the Professional Footballers' Association, commented about the growth of racism on the terraces: 'It seems that those who are directing abuse at black players are better organised. They remain the minority but they seem to have got together at clubs to make their voices heard. 99

In 1988, when Birmingham-born Mark Walters was signed by the top soccer club Glasgow Rangers for £1 million, he became the first black footballer to play in the Scottish League – and was taunted by some whites in the crowd who threw bananas on the pitch. Such abuse was widespread. A year earlier, in his annual report as Chairman of the Sports Council, John Smith had noted:

66 Racial abuse remains a problem, and it is deeply disappointing to note its spread from football to other sports – particularly at a time when so many of our black sportsmen and women are bringing such credit to their sports. 99

At the end of the 1980s these black sports stars included many who were the best in Britain at their event: Molly Samuel (karate), Notting Hill's double Olympic champion Francis Morgan 'Daley' Thompson (decathlon), Cardiff-born Colin Jackson (hurdles), John Regis (200 m), Dalton Grant (high jump), Stewart Falconer (long jump), Judy Simpson (heptathlon). Indeed the sprint ace Linford Christie received the MBE after captaining the British athletics squad that won the European Cup in 1989. If black stars were rare in sports that were expensive or practised mostly in private clubs – skiing, gliding, sailing, motor racing, motor cycling, golf, rowing – they were not so in sports taught in inner-city schools, such as netball, boxing, judo, basketball (at which Birmingham-born policeman Kevin Penny was an ace) and table tennis, at which Desmond Douglas, MBE, was the national champion for a decade. In some schools black children were even encouraged to practise sport at the expense of their exam results, as boxer Herol Graham and sprinter Mickey Morris remembered in *Black sportsmen* (1982) by E. Cashmore.

In 1991, London-born rugby league winger Martin Offiah scored a record number of tries, while Ellery Hanley, MBE, delighted his fans in Lancashire as well as those in Nevis and St Kitts by continuing to captain Wigan and Great Britain. By now several Afro-Caribbeans had played cricket for England, and Jeremy Guscott was England's latest superstar in rugby union. As for football, there were now so many stars (Barnes, Rocastle, Walters, Davis, Ince, Thomas, Walker, Parker, Daley, Elliott . . .) that as a team they might be as good as the current England XI. Only, how would the fans react if the manager selected an all-black eleven? Would it matter – if they were the

John Barnes, the Liverpool and England football star, back-heeling a banana.

At the Commonwealth Games in 1990 Diane Edwards (left) and Ann Williams won gold and silver respectively in the 800 metres.

best? Or what if the manager was black? Garth Crooks, one of Britain's first black football stars, was already Chairman of the Professional Footballers' Association.

In Britain in 1988 a poll of black and white youths, when asked which men they would most like to be, put the African-American film star Eddie Murphy in 2nd place and at the top, in 1st place, sports star Daley Thompson.

Trinidadian-born barrister Leonard Woodley became Britain's first Afro-Caribbean QC in 1988, a year ahead of Jamaican-born John Perry. Like Dr Alcindor (see page 47) Woodley still found time for cricket. 'Some people are probably against you because you are black', he said. 'But when it comes to cricket and you play well, people tend to forget about their prejudice.'

Guardsman Richard Stokes on duty outside Buckingham Palace, 1988. A sign that the Royal Family wanted more equality? (In fact, Stokes was subjected to so much racism that he left the army in 1991.)

How far?

Britain's first black police officer, the first black to play football for a British club ... whenever a new 'first' for the black community occurs, there are always two ways of looking at it. Each is a further step along the road to equality. At the same time, it reminds everybody how far there is still to go. As one community leader said:

66 Before we can claim we're making progress, we have to get beyond the point where we can single out each successful black by name. 99

Moreover, how long after the first black footballer before Britain has its first black football manager? How long after the first black policeman before the first black Chief Constable?

Marching on

Blacks have served in Britain's wars for centuries, including the American War of Independence, the Crimean War, two World Wars, the Falklands War, the Gulf War and in Northern Ireland. They have fought, they have won medals and they have died. Yet they have never been the most senior officers – these have always been white; and up to 1986, when Prince Charles noticed no black faces at the Trooping of the Colour, certain elite British regiments had never accepted one single black recruit. Then, in 1987, Richard Stokes became the first black to join the Grenadier Guards – and in 1988 he was on sentry duty outside Buckingham Palace. This was a breakthrough; and Guardsman Stokes had achieved a personal success. However, the wider question arose: was this a reason for other British blacks to be content with the pace of progress? After all, in the USA in 1987, a black New Yorker of Jamaican-born parents, General Colin Powell, had been promoted to the top post in the US army. In 1989 he became the USA's most senior officer of all: Chairman of the Joint Chiefs of Staff. In the US forces there were now 40 black generals and admirals. 'In time, that will not be something one should take note of at all', General Powell said. Yet in Britain there was not one senior black officer – nor any black in the senior grades of the Civil Service.

A normal achievement?

In 1986, a Sheffield newspaper editor, Michael Corner of *The Star*, described a problem that faces the media:

66 My own paper carried a picture story of the first black woman bus driver and that led to a debate in the offices as to why we had done it. The first bus driver, of course, is a story. The first woman bus driver, of course, is a story. But by highlighting the black driver, are we discriminating by saying this is odd? Or are we contributing to racial harmony by pointing out that the black woman driver is doing a normal job, in normal circumstances and making a normal achievement? 99

Would Britain's 'first black princess' be a suitable news story? Or the 'first black editor of a national newspaper'?

Still in Babylon?

One of Lord Scarman's findings in 1981 had been that young blacks in the inner cities needed jobs. In 1984 he toured Brixton again. What had changed? Between 1981 and 1984, Brixton's unemployment rate had doubled! In 1989 Lord Scarman said:

66 As a temporary phase, Afro-Caribbeans need an attitude in employers which will say: if you are as good an applicant, three times out of five we'll give the job to a black. 99

The later 1980s were profitable for people in certain types of work, overall unemployment fell, and some individual Afro-Caribbeans did well. But joblessness remained high among young blacks, and few black families left the inner cities. Many of those in work were in low-paid manual jobs, where – throughout the decade up to 1989 – wage increases did not keep pace with rising prices, least of all with house prices in leafy suburbs. Something else kept blacks in 'their' areas, too. In 1987 two TV reporters, one black, one white, filmed evidence of a colour bar still operating in Bristol, keeping blacks from jobs and from rented rooms in smarter areas. In Leicester in 1989 the Commission for Racial Equality was checking reports of an agent for some new houses who said, 'We don't want any blacks up here'.

In 1988 Enoch Powell claimed Britain was still threatened with 'violence on a scale which can only be described as civil war'. There were others with views like his. In December 1989, Tony Marlow, a white MP opposed to immigration from Hong Kong, said:

66 Vast areas of our inner cities have already been colonised by alien peoples with little commitment to our society or our way of life. There may be little blood flowing in the Tiber as yet. But all the most likely scenarios are filled with much foreboding. 99

Blacks had escaped their chains, but they were still in 'Babylon'. However talented or well qualified an individual was, he or she remained 'visible' and was exposed to prejudice that could turn brutal at any time – or be

In 1989, Norman Tebbit, MP, a former Cabinet Minister and ex-chairman of the Conservative Party, said:
'The former immigrants, the British Asians and British Caribbeans, have settled in well. But it's a pity that the issue of immigration should be re-opened, because most whites in Britain don't want to live in a multicultural, multiracial society.'

almost polite. In 1989 Hilda Amoo-Gottfried, a black lawyer, described with wry humour how, when she arrived at court for her cases, ushers would ask her: 'Are you a witness or will you be appearing in the dock?'

Some signs of hope

As the 1980s ended, there were also some hopeful signs. A study was published in 1989 that showed Afro-Caribbean pupils, on average, no longer lagging behind whites in exam results: they were behind in maths, but ahead in English. Government leaflets encouraged blacks to become school governors. There were four black MPs in the House of Commons now, too, who could ensure that black voices were heard. Indeed, immediately after his election, in a moving reference to his African roots, Paul Boateng said:

66 Some of us in this room have been waiting over 400 years for this moment. 99

Universities had been instructed to monitor the number of black applicants getting places; and the Prime Minister had said she wanted to do something for inner cities. Unemployment among blacks was still high, but some vital

An advertisement in *Just Seventeen* 13 March 1991, one of Britain's most popular magazines for teenagers.

Right. A leading article in *The Sun* on 8 June, 1991

placing advertisements in Trinidad's newspapers for nurses.

Moving ahead?

Whenever a new judge was to be appointed, other judges recommended 'most warmly people like themselves – successful, white, male, and middle-aged', wrote Sir William Goodhart, QC, in 1989. In a 1989 opinion poll two out of three people in Britain believed that police officers bent the rules in order to achieve convictions. But key changes were afoot, encouraging blacks to hope for fair treatment at the hands of the law. The new Lord Chancellor, Lord Mackay, had set up a programme of race awareness training for magistrates; and a 1988 report showing discrimination within prisons was being studied. In 1989 too, tens of thousands of pounds in compensation were paid by the police to black people including Ace Kelly (see page 72).

By now courts had convicted several police officers who had harassed blacks and this might deter other officers in future. In February 1989, in a move that could help to promote better relations, William Trant, director of the West Indian Standing Conference, urged 'black youngsters who participate in stealing, mugging or other crimes of violence to desist from such activities. Such anti-social behaviour casts a slur on the rest of the black community'. By 1989 the number of police officers from the visible ethnic minorities had risen to 1271, about 1.1 per cent of all officers; and fresh efforts to gain more black recruits included new-style advertisements in the press and a recruitment video in which Gary Wilmot, a black comedian, appeared. This was progress, even if relations between Afro-Caribbeans and the police continued to be strained.

diversification had taken place – Afro-Caribbeans were established in more types of jobs than ever before as indicated when, in 1988, Jamaican-born Yvonne Richards, a sales manager with *Reader's Digest*, was named as 'Corporate Businesswoman of the Year'. Black-owned small businesses existed, too. Moreover, the 30 per cent dip in the number of young people due to leave school in the 1990s would make employers think twice before turning away well-qualified blacks. Already, job adverts in some sectors were aimed directly at attracting applicants from the visible minorities. In 1989 a shortage of staff had led one local authority to recruit teachers directly from Barbados, while a hospital in Surrey was busy

Who's next?

WELL done, Bill Morris.

At 52, he becomes leader of Britain's biggest union, the Transport and General.

He will be our first black union boss. Proof that colour is no bar to public office.

Who will be the first black Prime Minister?

Fears of prejudice within the courts rose again in 1989, with the news that a senior Old Bailey judge, Sir James Miskin, QC, speaking at the Mansion House, had described an Afro-Caribbean man as a 'nig-nog'. However, Sir James retired not long after this.

In October 1990 the new minister for race relations at the Home Office, Angela Rumbold, MP, encouraged greater hope. She said:

66 The (Conservative) Government wants as many Asians, Afro-Caribbeans, and other ethnic minorities as possible to play a full part in national life. This is happening more and more. This doesn't mean there is anything wrong in those groups maintaining their own traditions and customs. 99

The final score?

To get to the heart of the history of Britain's Afro-Caribbean community and appreciate its meaning for the present and the future, society must listen to what black people today have to say, always bearing in mind that the view of any one individual, whether black or white, cannot be 'typical' but must be unique. Since most whites in Britain have no black neighbours, they might need to go out of their way to do this. Compared to the journeys made by the Afro-Caribbeans, from the 'middle passage' to Britain's inner cities, it would be but a short step. They might even learn something about themselves.

Sam King, who came to Britain in 1948 on the SS *Empire Windrush* and later became Mayor of Lambeth, said in 1988:

66 We are still having humiliation. But for every third of the average English people who are unreasonable to us there is another third who will go out of their way to help you. The other third couldn't care less as long as their football team plays on Saturdays and they can get their beer in the pubs! 99

Amon Saba Saakana, Trinidadian-born author of *Blues Dance* (1986), a novel about a Rastafarian in London, said:

66 I am hopeful about what could be done in Britain. The kids here are beginning to mix. There is still a chance in Britain of a fair and egalitarian society. Increasingly now black and white kids are friends. 99

In 1990, Clive Walker (see page 55) said:
'I must say, though, that there's favouritism and prejudice in every society, in the West Indies, too, not just here in Britain. And you do best if you look for the good in people. You can find that everywhere, too.'

History has now come full circle. Bristol's merchants specialised in supplying slaves for Jamaica's plantations. Now the descendant of a Jamaican slave has been elected to Bristol's top position...

When racism does not interfere, blacks can take up issues that benefit everyone. In 1987, 16-year-old bird-watcher Lester Holloway, seen here with actress Toyah Wilcox, won the 'Best of British Youth' award for his campaign to save a wildlife area from being turned into a rail depot for the Channel Tunnel.

In 1990 a former bus conductor, Jim Williams, became the first-ever black Lord Mayor of Bristol, as Jamaica's *Sunday Gleaner* noted on 29 July 1990.

Index